THE
BODY ART
BOOK

D0390519

Most Berkley Books are available at special quantity discounts for bulk purchases for sales promotions, premiums, fund-raising, or educational use. Special books or book excerpts can also be created to fit specific needs.

For details, write to Special Markets, The Berkley Publishing Group, 375 Hudson Street, New York, New York 10014.

THE BODY ART BOOK

A COMPLETE, ILLUSTRATED GUIDE
TO TATTOOS, PIERCINGS, AND
OTHER BODY MODIFICATIONS

Jean-Chris Miller

Illustrations by Denise de la Cerda

BERKLEY BOOKS, NEW YORK

This book stresses the need for safety precautions, the use of an experienced body art practitioner, and the importance of proper tools and techniques. Even if the cautionary advice is followed, tattoos, piercings, and other body modifications involve physical risk. The author and publisher specifically disclaim responsibility for any adverse effects or unforeseen consequences resulting from the use of any information contained herein and do not endorse any of the body art practitioners listed in this book. The reader is advised to consult his or her physician immediately if any complications arise.

This book is an original publication of The Berkley Publishing Group.

THE BODY ART BOOK

A Berkley Book / published by arrangement with
the author

PRINTING HISTORY
Berkley trade paperback edition / October 1997

All rights reserved.
Copyright © 1997 by Jean-Chris Miller.
Text illustrations © 1997 by Denise de la Cerda.
Text design by Irving Perkins Associates.
This book may not be reproduced in whole or in part,
by mimeograph or any other means, without permission.
For information address: The Berkley Publishing Group, a division
of Penguin Putnam Inc., 375 Hudson Street, New York,
New York 10014.

The Penguin Putnam Inc. World Wide Web site address is
http://www.penguinputnam.com

ISBN: 0-425-15985-X

BERKLEY®
Berkley Books are published by The Berkley Publishing Group,
a division of Penguin Putnam Inc.,
375 Hudson Street, New York, New York 10014.
BERKLEY and the "B" design
are trademarks belonging to Penguin Putnam Inc.

PRINTED IN THE UNITED STATES OF AMERICA

10 9 8 7

*This book is dedicated to Casey Exton,
who has tirelessly championed body art
and artists for many years.*

ACKNOWLEDGMENTS

I WOULD LIKE TO thank the following people for their support, advice, and inspiration: Denise de la Cerda, Anil Gupta, Dennis Feliciano, Myke Maldonado, Maya, Mike Martin, Artie Richard, Albert Sgambati, Mike Sirot, the crew at Streamline Tattoos, Nick Wiggins; my body art partners-in-crime: Amy Becker, Annemarie Fasulo, Tony Romel Garcia, Ken Knabb, Dan Levine, Brenda Mercado, Victoria Minervini, and Marco Turelli; Tom, Judy, Scott & Sean Miller, and Jean Demuth.

CONTENTS

Introduction   1

1: A Brief History of Body Art   7

2: Styles of Body Art   16

3: Why We Do It   28

4: Learning the Language   37

5: Getting Good Work   76

6: Safety First   87

7: Procedure and Aftercare   94

8: How to Find the Right Artist   107

9: Mehndi, Scarification, and Other Practices   114

10: Getting Rid of Your Work   122

Appendix: International Directory of Body Art   127

INTRODUCTION

BODY ART IS EVERYWHERE these days. Tattoo designs are exhibited in galleries; pierced belly buttons are trendy among fashion models; Greek symbols are traditionally branded into fraternity brothers' skin. It seems as if the whole world has rediscovered the ancient art of decorating one's body with permanent marks.

These permanent marks are part of what define us as human beings. They are a means of self-expression and a vehicle of self-awareness, two qualities that separate us from other living things on this planet. No other animal decorates itself—and decoration is just one aspect of body art. Tattooing, piercing, and other adornments have been used for centuries in rites of passage, in religious rituals, or as a form of tribal identification—in *all* cultures.

Sometimes they're emblems that commemorate special events in a person's life. Many different tribes of Asian women shared the tradition of getting tattooed during pregnancy. The reasons for the tattoos varied, from protecting mother and child against demonic possession to influencing the baby's sex, but the end result was always the same: a permanent souvenir of a life-changing moment. This is also why many religious pilgrimages are documented with a sacred tattoo.

The fact that these designs are permanent also reminds the wearer that she is changed forever. Thus, the worldwide association of tattooing, cutting, branding, etc., as a rite of

1

passage. Because these procedures involve some degree of pain (much more in the past than now), they show the wearer to be strong and fearless.

Occasionally tattoos are clan markings that identify a person with a particular group. For example, some pre-Christian European cultures believed that when a person died, unless he bore the mark of his tribe, he'd wander around in the next world searching aimlessly for his own kind, throughout eternity. Tattoos were used to mark a person's clan affiliations in *this* world so that he could find (and be found by) other members of his clan in the next one.

Tattooing is by far the most popular kind of permanent body decoration, and is now considered a respected form of "folk art"—art created by the common people, for the common people, reflecting their particular traditions and culture. Unlike other body adornments, which are ruled by the whims of fashion—baby-blue or gunmetal-gray fingernail polish, long sideburns, short sideburns, no sideburns—tattooing is based completely on what *you* are into and think is cool, beautiful, or appropriate.

And unlike nail polish or hairstyles, which are temporary ways of revealing your personality, a tattoo is forever. That's why it's so important that the tattoo you choose be one you'll be happy with and proud of for the rest of your life (and beyond—tattoos are still clearly visible on mummies, even after five thousand years!). It must be a good design, placed properly on your body, be the right size, and most important, it must be done well. Remember, it will be there forever, so there's really no such thing as taking too long to decide what you want, where you want it, and whom you want to do it. Tattooing is a unique and artistic way to show the world what you're all about.

Piercing is another form of expression that's very creative and individualized—and also pretty permanent. You can remove the jewelry, but the hole will remain for quite some time, so, like tattooing, it requires planning and knowledge to get something you'll always enjoy. Nor do you want to walk around with the wrong kind of jewelry in your piercing. You may think it's very cool to have that giant ring hanging from your septum, flapping over the top of your lips, but are your friends whispering *"toro, toro!"* behind your back? Nothing complements a face better than a well-placed piercing, one that's not too big or too small. That little gleam of metal adds character, mystery, and undeniable sex appeal. And don't let anyone tell you piercing is some weird, new craze; piercing and other body arts have always been a part of humankind's beauty vocabulary.

Today, in our Western culture, we're witnessing a renewed interest in tattooing, piercing, and other body modifications. Although these practices have always been around, they've usually bounced back and forth between acceptability and outsider status, depending on the cultural climate of any given period. During the Victorian era, for example, a time of public purity and private debauchery, it was fashionable for society women to have their nipples pierced. Yet the children and grandchildren of those Victorian women would have considered these matriarchs downright uncivilized, just as the great-great-grandchildren of those same ladies probably see nothing wrong with their, if you will, titillating decorations. In the past twenty years, the body art movement has exploded. The art itself has reached creative and technical heights never before imagined, and permanent personal decoration is gaining wider popularity.

Despite the long and important history of body art, some say tattooing is just a trend that will disappear in a few years. But with an estimated one out of every eleven people in the United States alone sporting some kind of ink, that hardly seems likely. Instead, we have reintroduced a means of expressing ourselves that can carry many levels of significance, both personally and culturally determined.

That's the difference between trendiness and timelessness—the significance and forethought you give the work. Something that requires such a big commitment (it's lifelong, it may hurt a little, you have to care for it to keep it looking good) requires a lot of planning. *Permanent body art is a big decision that will affect the rest of your life.*

There's a revolution in personal style happening now; high-fashion designers take their cues from funky streetwear while street kids flaunt their designer labels. These unforeseen convergences are breaking down the class stereotypes associated with a certain "look"—as the rules of style give way to individual taste. The unique and intimate nature of body art provides a means to express this individuality—something that's becoming pretty hard to do these days. In an age of the shop-at-home/bank-at-home/work-at-home lifestyle, it's very easy to feel that we are little more than a series of digits: credit-card numbers, E-mail addresses, PINs. Our neighborhoods and cities are losing their distinct flavors; one area looks so much like the next, it's as if the planet is becoming one big strip mall. There is little sense of community and even less cultural identification. On top of it all, we are faced with an increasing loss of personal freedoms, as more and more areas of our lives become regulated by the government. Wearing seat belts, getting immunization shots, or recycling our newspapers—these are no longer our decisions. It's easy to see how all of this could make us feel we're something less than unique individuals.

Certain folks use body art as a way to reclaim some of the customs and magic of their ancestors, or to symbolize important occasions or transitions in their lives. Some want to adorn themselves in ways *they* think are attractive; their definition of beauty is not the blond-haired, blue-eyed one that they see in *Vogue* or *GQ*—it's something wilder, more exotic. Others just want to shock and amaze the neighbors. Whatever the reason, tattooing, piercing, and the rest of the body arts can be very powerful for two reasons. *They give us control over our own bodies and they express things about our inner selves that words alone often cannot articulate.*

Permanent body art is a dramatic and artistic way to show the world something about your personality—and the fact that this art is slightly unconventional and somewhat daring only adds to its appeal. There are so many possibilities and variations to tattooing and piercing that it can all seem overwhelming. In fact, learning about these possibilities is half the fun. As you become more familiar with the rich history and endless variety of tattooing, piercing, and other forms of body art and body modifications, you'll see just how creative and meaningful they can be.

There are also some very real health concerns you must be aware of before letting anyone come near you with a needle. Most significant is knowing how diseases are transmitted and what precautions the artist you choose must take to prevent contamination. But there are also infections, allergies, and other sensitivities to consider, all of which we will cover in this book. You play as great a part in assuring successful work as the person you choose to execute it does—ultimately, your body art is *your* responsibility.

This book will give you the information necessary to get the best and safest tattoo or piercing possible. It's written so that you can access data easily and quickly. You'll be able to refer to it again and again, because it covers everything from planning your design, to choosing your artist, through aftercare, and much, much more—everything you need to become a walking, talking work of art!

CHAPTER 1
A BRIEF HISTORY
OF BODY ART

THE MOST ANCIENT TATTOOED specimen, to date, is that of the "Iceman," a Bronze Age man uncovered after being frozen in a glacier on the Tyrolean Alps (between Austria and Italy) since about 3300 B.C. A tattooed band of stripes was found on his lower back, a simple cross behind his left knee, and more stripes on his right ankle. The tattoos could have been ornamental, or perhaps they marked his status in his tribe. They may have been healing or protective talismans whose purpose was to prevent pain in those areas of his body.

We know of many examples of tattooing in ancient Egypt, the oldest found on the mummy of an Egyptian priestess, Amunet, who lived approximately four thousand years ago. Because of her religious status, some archaeologists have speculated that her body art had spiritual or magical connotations. Others feel the designs were of a sexual nature.

Another female mummy from roughly the same period has both tattoos and decorative scarification. It's been theorized that her body adornments enhanced her sexual attractiveness and/or were talismans to ensure her fertility.

There's also evidence of piercing in ancient Egypt. A statue of Akhenaton, dating back to about 1400 B.C., depicts what many consider to be a navel piercing on the famous pharaoh. The sculptor carved out a hole above the navel from which, most likely, hung some kind of golden jewelry. As is the case with many ancient artifacts, that jewelry was stolen centuries ago.

In countries where people have dark skin (which generally doesn't show tattoo pigments well), branding, piercing, scarification, and other elaborate body modifications have been practiced for centuries—and still are. The variety and uniqueness of body modifications found in these places is fascinating. Elongating the neck by adding a series of copper rings, inserting plates in the lip, and greatly stretched earlobes are just a few of the practices still seen in Africa, Central and South America, Asia, and Southeast Asia.

Greek and Roman civilizations are atypical in their lack of permanent body adornment, although there is evidence of tattooing for tribal identification in ancient Rome, as well as piercing during the first century A.D. Some historians believe nipple piercing was used as a mark of rank among the centurions, a class of Roman military officers. It's even rumored that the centurions used their nipple piercings to fasten their heavy capes in place! What better way to show your physical superiority and ability to withstand pain than by attaching your clothing directly onto your chest. Mucho macho, centurion!

Some of the most diverse, ornate, and bizarre body art this planet has ever seen was found in the mysterious, complex world of the Maya. This civilization thrived in southeast Mexico, Guatemala, and Belize and reached its apex between 300 and 900 A.D. Mayan body modifications are among the most extreme, not only in the particular practices and the reasoning behind them, but in their incredible variety.

For the Maya, body modifications, whether temporary or permanent, were done for spiritual reasons as well as beautification. At different times throughout their history, Mayan people favored various placements for their body art, but seen as a whole, there is practically no area that was not the focus of some kind of modification or adornment.

Full body tattoos, even facial tattoos, were acquired by men and women. Scarification was practiced by both sexes. Ears, nose, lips, navel, and genitals were all pierced, and often the holes were stretched bigger and bigger over time. Surface-to-surface piercings were done on the forehead, temples, arms, and legs. Teeth were filed to sharp points and inlaid with precious gems.

The Maya's extravagant modifications started at birth, when balls were hung between children's eyes to make them cross-eyed. Babies were also fitted with wooden molds on their foreheads to reshape them into a continuous slope that started at the bridge of the nose and angled back to the top of the head. Crossed eyes and sloping foreheads were considered highly attractive features that every Maya struggled to attain. Theirs is just one example of how different cultures use body art and body modification to achieve *their own idea of beauty.*

Sometimes body art was used as a defense tactic. Just as you might think twice before getting in the way of a big biker with skulls tattooed all over his body and a thick ring through his nose, so did our ancestors ponder doing battle with wild tribes who had, as an example, blue skin (think *Braveheart*). British warriors stained themselves with woad (blue dye made from a mustard plant), and cut patterns into their skins, basically to psych out their opponents. Others used tattooing and scarification as a way to show to which tribe they belonged. The Picts, who inhabited northern Britain, are so named because of the pictures tattooed on their skins.

Just as occurred in other cultures with tattoo traditions, when these pagan tribes were "converted" to the Christian religion, their spiritual and cultural rites (which included tattooing, piercing, and scarification) were outlawed. This banishment of body art stems from a passage in the Old Testament, Leviticus 19:28, which states, "Ye shall not make any cuttings in your flesh for the dead, nor print any marks upon you." How this decree against mutilating yourself in memory of the dead was interpreted to include all tattoos is anybody's guess. For those of you who follow the spiritual laws of the Old Testament, keep in mind that Leviticus 19:27 states: "Ye shall not round the corners of your head, neither shall thou mar the corners of thy beard." No tattoos, no haircuts.

As the period of the Crusades gave way to the Inquisition, it became a serious offense to have tattoos because it meant the wearer had been involved in another religion. While these and other body modifications continued to be practiced underground as a way for non-Christian people to identify each other, God forbid you got caught and your mark was revealed. Well, according to Señor Torquemada and his cohorts of the Spanish Inquisition, God *did* forbid it.

Tattoos remained an archaic taboo until their reintroduction to the Western world in the late eighteenth century by way of a British exploration to chart "undiscovered" lands.

Captain James Cook, in his ship the *Endeavor,* set sail on August 16, 1768, planning to circumnavigate the globe. During his three-year journey, he visited many islands of the Pacific Ocean, most of which included tattooing as part of their culture. It's Cook who gave us the word we spell as "tattoo," based on similar words in Polynesian cultures that were used to describe the practice.

On board the *Endeavor* was Sir Joseph Banks, a British botanist. Along with cataloging many types of animal and plant life, Banks documented the indigenous cultures at every stop along the way. Included in these notes are many references to tattooing, which are important not only historically, but also helped rekindle interest in the practice in Europe. When the *Endeavor* returned to England in 1771, Banks disembarked with a permanent memento of his voyage: the first tattoo on a modern Western man!

One of the tattooing cultures Banks wrote about was that of the Maori (of Polynesian-Melanesian descent) of New Zealand. The Maoris' tattooing custom is a facial decoration called *Moko*. It's an ancient practice that connects the wearers with their ancestors. By the patterns tattooed on a Maori's face, you could tell everything you needed to know about him: his rank in the community, who his father was, even how many times he'd been married. Indigenous peoples from all over the world have long used intricate tattoo designs to convey information about themselves, although sometimes the process of getting the tattoos was so dangerous (extremely painful and prone to infection) that the wearer became very ill and died.

The Samoan tattoo tradition of Pe'a is notorious for its excruciating pain. The great majority of the ink was concentrated in the area from the waist to just below the knees, and the design involved many intricate lines and patterns. The process was a lengthy one. With a mallet in one hand, the tattooist pounded the ink in the skin by means of a comblike tool made of bone. Surviving the Pe'a tattooing process was a sign of a person's strength and stamina, to say the least.

The sailors that traveled the globe in the eighteenth and nineteenth centuries were responsible for the resurgence of tattoos in European cultures. Seamen returned from their exotic travels with stories of abduction and forced tattooing. In the early 1800s, it was a fad among the European upper classes to get tiny tattoos as a way to vicariously live a small bit of the wild stories these men would tell—even though the veracity of these tales is highly questionable.

Soon a few sailors found themselves the darlings of the salon society. They would entertain rich people at private parties with stories of danger and adventure, made all the more believable by the strange tribal tattoos they sported. Western societies' fascination with tattooed people was exploited by circuses and traveling sideshows—many a retired sea dog made a bundle posing as a "Live Wild Man." But by the late 1800s, tattooed people were so common on the traveling show circuit that promoters had to go to greater extremes to attract the crowds. Entire tattooed families would be exhibited, and if that wasn't enough, even their tattooed pets would be put on display! By the turn of the century, audiences had seen tattooed people (and animals) of every kind, so shows added "geeking" (bizarre acts like swallowing worms or biting the heads off chickens) and exotic talents, like sword swallowing or pounding nails into the nose, to their side attractions' repertoire.

The custom of sailors (and all branches of servicemen) getting tattooed continues to this day. Traditional seafaring tattoos are still around, and have roots that go back more than a hundred years. Seamen are commonly known as superstitious folk. Many of the "sailor" tattoos still seen today have roots in seafarers' mysticism. Those tattoos were for protection, remembrance, or to symbolize a voyage. A rooster tattooed on one foot and a pig tattooed on the other was believed to prevent a man from drowning. Swallows, still a common tattoo symbol, served to help a sailor navigate the seas and make sure he made it home. They also served as markers for time spent traveling. One swallow meant the sailor had logged at least five thousand miles at sea, and each additional swallow represented another five hundred miles. Other traditional symbols indicated the sailor had crossed the equator (Neptune/Poseidon, Greco-Roman god of the sea) or the international dateline (a dragon).

Also, tattoos were a good way to recognize a person who may have died an ugly death in battle. Having this indelible mark meant that your body could be identified and sent home. This is similar to the way we now use such things as dental X rays as a key to identity—or fingerprints, DNA, or police records.

On December 8, 1891, the first electric tattoo machine was registered by its inventor, Samuel O'Reilly, at the United States Patent Office. It was based on a machine patented by Thomas Edison in 1875, but rather than using the tool as a means to embroider fabric, which Edison did, O'Reilly's tattoo machine was meant to "embroider" skin. He began working out of a barbershop in New York City, calling his business a "tattoo parlor"—the first such enterprise in the United States.

Soon tattoo parlors were springing up all over the country—mainly in port towns to serve their naval clientele. During the First and Second World Wars, different branches of the military adopted the sailors' tradition of tattooing as a means of mystical protection, a souvenir or remembrance, or just to show what badasses they were!

The prison tradition of tattooing springs from these same motives. Inmates' permanent marks showed the world they were fearless and not to be toyed with (serving a purpose much like ancient warriors' body art). A whole style of tattooing, *Jailhouse* or *Black and Gray* (so named because the work was generally rendered in the available black ink), evolved from prison tattooing. Many books have been written about the secret language of prison tattoos all over the world.

In the mid-1970s, for the first time ever, tattooists began holding tattoo conventions. Ink slingers and ink lovers from all over converged as a group to talk shop and show off their work. These gatherings changed the course of modern body art. Up until that point, tattooing was a very secretive craft, and tattooists guarded their techniques, their equipment, and their territory ferociously. It was impossible to "break into the business"; no one would teach an outsider anything. If you were lucky enough to be taught how to tattoo by an old-timer, you were virtually an indentured servant to that person, working for him until he retired or died. Should you attempt to start your own tattoo business, you would be run out of town, your shop burned to the ground, and your hands broken to ensure you wouldn't be able to tattoo again—and that's if you were lucky! This territorial aspect of tattooing persists, in varying degrees, to this day.

Slowly, due to conventions, magazines, and other kinds of exposure, tattooing began to emerge from the underground. People started to recognize its artistic merit and folk-art roots and to see that skin art could be worn by more than just convicts, sailors, and carnival people. Its exotic and erotic qualities appealed to a generation obsessed with liberating their bodies and their minds, as well as rejecting all things conventional and "square."

In the early 1980s, fine art discovered tattooing. Artists like Ed Paschke and Tony Fitzgerald began using tattoo imagery in their paintings. Others began exploring tattooing itself as a medium of expression. The interest of fine artists in tattooing helped not only to legitimize it in many people's eyes, but also expanded tattooing's creative vocabulary—there was an explosion of styles and imagery. This is referred to as the *New School*—the period when tattooists started to consider their craft an art form, and began to share their knowledge with others while constantly pushing the limits of tattoo technology.

The body-art revolution had begun.

With the arrival of tattoo magazines and annual conventions, body art began reaching millions of people who would have never before considered it a legitimate means of expression. In 1989, Re/Search Publications put out a book called *Modern Primitives*, which introduced the world to a California man who calls himself Fakir Musafar. Musafar has been exploring (and documenting) body adornments and rituals since his youth. His personal history includes piercing, tattooing, suspension by hooks, neck stretching, waist cinching, and scarification—virtually any form of body modification known to humankind. Fakir Musafar now operates a school of body modification in San Francisco, and is generally considered to be on the cutting edge of the piercing movement—the "Godfather of Hole."

The influence of Musafar's exploration of other cultures' body adornments, plus the influence of such movie figures as the futuristic savages in *Mad Max* and the biomechanical hybrids in *Hellraiser* and the *Alien* movies, turned "Modern

Primitives" into a full-blown movement, which incorporates past traditions of many cultures, current social and political concerns, and futuristic visions of the human race.

As you can see from this brief history, body art is somewhat cyclical in nature. Today we're experiencing one of the biggest revivals ever. The combination of technology, historical awareness, and artistic ability have taken body art to heights never before imagined. It's exciting to wonder just how far it can evolve. More than part of our past, body art is part of our present and our future.

CHAPTER 2

STYLES OF
BODY ART

TATTOOS

TATTOOING IS AN EXPRESSIVE, dramatic, and diverse art. Tattoo imagery is limitless—the only boundary is your imagination. The more you know about the options available to you, the more informed your decision will be about what design or image you want to wear forever.

Most tattooists specialize in a certain style of tattooing, the fundamentals of which can be summarized as three basic approaches: *Flat,* which is characterized by a lack of detail; *Traditional* (and *Neotraditional*), which is known for thick, black outlines and solid blocks of color; and *Fine Line,* which is distinguished by narrower, finer lines and greater detail. The first step in figuring out what kind of tattoo you want is choosing which of these techniques most pleases you.

Flat Tats

Flat tattooing employs solid blocks of color (often in black) with no shading, detailing, or texturing of any sort. Shapes and simple symbols are tattooed in one thick line (think of the

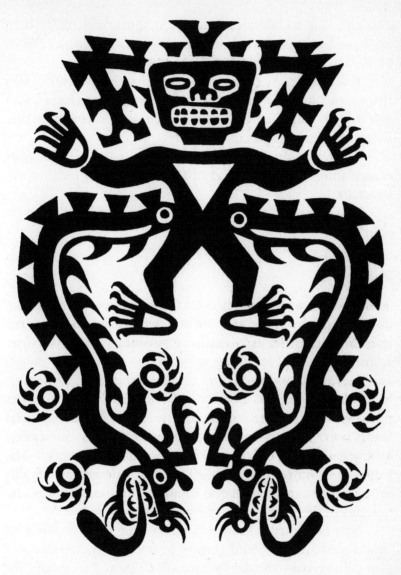

biohazard symbol or a music note), and can be filled in or left
as an outline.

Flat tattooing is perhaps best represented by the *Tribal*
style. This (also called *New Tribal*) is a catchall title for many
different styles found all over the world. From Alaska to New

Zealand, Asia to Nicaragua, simple designs rendered in dark ink have been used to show a person's status, protect from harm, and enhance appearance.

Tribal takes two basic forms: *Geometric* (which uses shapes such as circles, squares, and triangles to create a cohesive overall design) and *Organic* (which uses flowing lines that follow the natural lines of the body).

Flat tattooing—if it's done well and complements your musculature—results in a very flattering, striking piece of abstract art.

The disadvantage is obvious: it's flat. A lump of color on your skin.

Traditional

Traditional (and its funkier cousin, Neotraditional) tattooing got its name from the kind of skin art that was done in the late 1800s into the early half of this century in the Western world. Traditional tattooing is based on clean, simple design and execution, and uses thick, black, outlines, filled in with solid blocks of color. There's little detail in the work apart from what is absolutely necessary to convey the design, and this is done with color and shading instead of more intricate outlines. Daggers, hearts, snakes, pinup girls, panthers, roses, eagles, and butterflies are all Traditional design motifs (although they can be rendered in any tattoo style, just as any design can be done in the Traditional style).

Neotraditional takes the imagery and aesthetic ideas of Traditional tattooing and throws in fine-arts techniques and pop-culture sass—the designs are a little more "cartoony." In Neotraditional tattooing, the skin that's *not* tattooed (called "negative space") is as important as the skin that *is* (a basic rule that applies to lots of tattoo designs); skilled shading and color layering give the work depth. Flat fill-in of an outline is *not* Neotraditional tattooing.

The advantages to modern Traditional tattooing are that the pieces are visually striking and they age well. These simple designs, with bold colors and thick outlines, are easy to "read." The consensus is that Traditional tattoos can be seen from great distances (as opposed to Fine Line work, which often requires much closer inspection in order to see the detail) and will still be visible years from now (whereas "busier" or more cluttered designs can turn to "mush" over time). The rule of thumb is: If it's bold, it will hold.

The potential problem with Traditional tattooing is that you could end up with a crude piece of work. Clean, simple work requires as much skill as more complicated work.

Fine Line

Modern Fine Line tattooing changed the nature of ink slinging. It expanded the imagery tremendously (virtually anything can be translated into a tattoo now) and opened the craft up to serious artistry. It's characterized by thin(ner) outlines, precise shading, and detailed designs. There is much

more focus on the lines of a tattoo. Using smaller needle configurations (the number of needles bunched together to create different tattoo effects)—single-needle to three- or occasionally five-needle setups—the tattooist can create complex work with delicate coloring, subtle highlights and undertones, intricate patterns, and realistic representations.

From *Portraiture* to *Black and Gray* to *Celtic*, the exactness of Fine Line allows for precision and intricacy in your tattoo. Complex shading gives the work more naturalistic shape, texture, and added dimension—the tattoo looks like it could jump right off of your skin!

The trick is to not cram too much into the design. Overdetailing will make the tattoo hard to read; and unlike other art mediums, *your* canvas is a living organism that will change through the years. It will wrinkle, sag, dry out, and change texture. Don't be swayed by overeager tattooists who say they can fit all two-hundred-plus bones in the human body into that tiny three-inch skeleton tattoo you want. Remember: *The more complicated the tattoo, the bigger it has to be.* That simple. A good Fine Line tattooist will give you a piece that lasts through the years—it's all a matter of skill.

A lot of tattooists combine the best of both worlds, incorporating the clean, solid blocks of color that characterize Traditional tattooing with the complex designs of Fine Line. The first step in choosing your tattoo is to decide which of these three basic approaches best suits you. This is the foundation for your choice of a design and of the tattooist who will realize it.

Within the context of Flat, Traditional, or Fine Line tattooing are grouped a number of different styles. For more on each of these styles, see the glossary of tattoo terminology contained in Chapter 4.

STYLES OF PIERCING

Piercing is an extremely popular form of body art these days. It can be understated and elegant, like a tiny nose ring; funky and fun, like a bunch of different piercing styles in the same ear; or radical and extravagant, like surface-to-surface piercings on the neck or hand. Whichever way you play it, you *must* go to a professional piercer. Not only are professional piercers trained in the areas of safety and health, they have an *aesthetic* understanding of piercing as well.

Body Jewelry: Styles, Metals, and Sizes

Just as important as choosing the right piercing professional is wearing the right jewelry. Many problems encountered with piercings, even after they're healed, result from putting the wrong kind of jewelry in the hole.

Professional body jewelry is hypoallergenic, which means it's unlikely to provoke an allergic reaction. The metals used are highly inert (they don't react readily with other chemical compounds) and oxide-resistant (exposure to oxygen, water, or bodily fluids will cause most metals to corrode from oxidization). Body jewelry comes in many different sizes and is measured not just by how big the ring or barbell is, but by how thick it is (called the *gauge*).

With a little education, you can create a unique personal statement with the jewelry you wear. Once your pierce has gone through the primary healing process, you're ready to explore the options!

Jewelry Styles

The design and manufacturing of body jewelry is in its infancy; new styles are being introduced to the market every day.

The most common pieces of body jewelry are the *bead ring,* a ring with a bead that screws in the ends, and the *captive bead ring,* which is just what it says: a ring fastened by a bead that is held in place—"captive"—by tension. Bead rings come in many shapes besides round. They can be teardrop-shaped, oval, or even square.

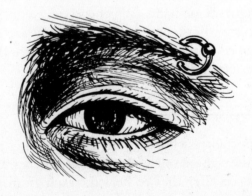

Another common body jewelry design is the *barbell*. This is a long post with beads that screw into both ends. Barbells

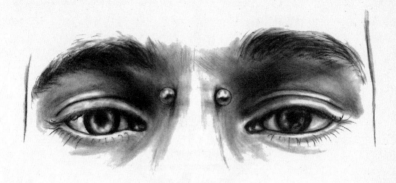

can be straight, curved, or circular. Some barbells have one flat end and one beaded end for piercings that go through the inside of your mouth; these are called *labret studs*. This way, the end of the barbell is flat inside your mouth with no pesky bead to annoy you.

There is a special stud for your nostril, called a *nostril screw*. The post of this stud is corkscrew-shaped, which prevents it from popping out. For a wilder look through your septum, try a *spike* or a *tusk*. For a (much) milder look, a *septum retainer* is used to maintain your septum piercing when you don't want to wear jewelry. This open-ended, horseshoe-shaped piece pivots back into your nostrils to hide your piercing.

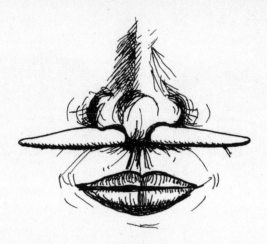

Some people stretch their piercings; they widen the holes by progressively inserting larger and larger gauges of jewelry. There are two kinds of special jewelry used in stretched piercings that really show off the size of the hole. The first is a *plug*, which is a cylindrical, solid piece that's held in place by a rubber ring on each end. A stretched hole can also be dec-

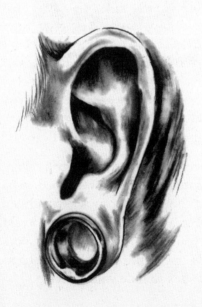

orated with a metal *earlet* (or *eyelet*), which is a hollow tube with flared ends—think of a thimble that's open on both ends. Earlets are also called *flesh tunnels,* an appropriate name because you can clearly see through their hollow center.

Jewelry Metals

A professional body piercer will offer you a wide selection of jewelry made from nonreactive metals. The most commonly used are *surgical stainless steel, niobium,* and *titanium.* To decrease the risk of infection or allergic reaction, and to ensure that your piercing heals properly, you *must* wear suitable jewelry, and that means one of the three above metals.

Surgical stainless steel should be of the highest grade, commonly referred to as "316-L"; this is the same grade surgeons use for implants in the body. It doesn't tarnish, it's scratch-resistant, and it's very strong, so it won't change shape. Of course it only comes in one color—silver—but the pieces that screw into the end of surgical-stainless-steel jewelry come in a variety of colors and shapes.

Niobium and titanium start out a silverish color, but through the process of anodization (electric currents and oxides are used to "coat" the surface, which then reflects a specific color when seen in the light), they can be produced in a rainbow of colors. There's a slightly greater risk of allergic reaction with niobium (but only if you suffer from extreme metal allergies already), but titanium is considered the least reactive metal that body jewelry can be made from. Both are corrosion-resistant and lightweight.

Gold and sterling silver should *never* be used for initial piercings. Some piercers do initial piercings with a high grade of gold (18K or higher), but since there is no such thing as "pure" gold, this is not recommended. All gold is mixed with other metals, which may cause an allergic reaction in people with metal sensitivities. It's fine to use once your piercing has healed.

Sterling silver, on the other hand, is not a good metal to stick in a piercing at any point. Because it's mixed with other metals and has a tendency to flake off, almost everyone will have a reaction to sterling silver in their fresh piercing. Even if you use it in a completely healed piercing, it will still oxidize and turn black (like sterling silverware does)—disgusting!

Platinum and its offshoot, palladium, are also great for body jewelry, but are not used as commonly because of their cost.

After your piercing is healed, you may want to try acrylic (plastic), glass, or organic (wood, bone) jewelry for more variety. They look great, but do carry a greater risk of infection because they're porous, which means pesky little bacteria and fungi can grow in them, and they can crack. Let your professional piercer determine whether or not your piercing is sufficiently healed before trying them out.

Jewelry Sizes

Body jewelry comes in many sizes, and is measured in terms of both thickness, by gauge, and of diameter (or length for straight jewelry). The thickness of jewelry is measured by the Brown & Sharpe gauging system; the smaller the gauge, the thicker the jewelry, thus a ten-gauge ring is much thicker than a sixteen-gauge. Initial piercings are usually done with a twenty, eighteen, sixteen, or occasionally a fourteen gauge. A professional piercer will determine the best gauge for your initial piercing based on where the jewelry is going to be placed and how you want it to look.

The diameter measures the distance inside a ring; this corresponds to length in the case of a barbell. Because certain piercings swell a great deal when you first get them, you will go through two or more sizes of jewelry. For the initial piercing, the piercer must select jewelry that is wide enough, in the case of a ring, or long enough, in the case of a barbell, to allow for any tissue inflammation. Once the swelling has subsided, you will *downsize* to a better-fitting piece of jewelry. A common example of downsizing is tongue piercings, which require at least two sizes of barbells—one size for the anticipated swelling and one for the final outcome.

Some people don't settle for the gauge of their piercing once it's healed. They keep stretching the hole, making it larger and larger. Stretching is a creative way to change the appearance of your piercing. If you start out with an eighteen or sixteen gauge, after the piercing is fully healed, you can go back and have your piercer insert a thicker gauge, such as a fourteen or a twelve. Once that size heals, you can go down even further, to a ten or an eight. You can gradually work your way down to a 00 gauge—and beyond! Another way of stretching your piercing is to use an *insertion taper,* which has a fine point on one end and gradually flares out; the thicker part is slowly pushed through your ear, widening your hole. Your professional piercer can also supply you with a weight to hang from your piercing that will have the same effect.

JEWELRY GAUGE CHART

| | Thickness in | |
Gauge	Inches	Millimeters
20	0.032	0.813
18	0.040	1.024
16	0.051	1.290
14	0.064	1.629
12	0.081	2.052
10	0.102	2.588
8	0.128	3.264
6	0.162	4.111
4	0.204	5.186
2	0.257	6.543
0	0.324	8.230
00	0.364	9.246

CHAPTER 3

WHY WE
DO IT

BODY ART IS A mode of self-expression that's been with us since
we developed the motor skills needed to hold the tools that
carved holes in our bodies. It's widely considered the *first* means
of visual expression. Early people cut open their skin and rubbed
soot into the wounds to mark themselves. They punctured their
skin with the bones and teeth of animals. They decorated themselves with scars that formed intricate patterns.

A common question asked of our ancestors' body marks
as well as our own is: Why do it? There are as many answers
to that question as there are styles of body art. Let's start with
the ancient body modifiers.

Maybe they marked themselves for defense; a person with
big black stripes on his face or a boar's tooth through his nose
could frighten an attacker off just by his appearance. They may
have used tattoos and scarification as an early form of magic; a
permanent symbol of the warm sun, for example, may have been
thought to help stave off the effects of a cold, dark night. They
could have shown spiritual devotion by "sacrificing" their flesh
to the gods or made permanent marks that signified tribal affil-
iation. It could have been a way of proving they were brave and
courageous warriors strong enough to stand the pain of ancient
body-art practices (a true test of stamina!). Or it's possible they
were just trying to improve their looks.

At some point in time, all of the above were reasons people got tattoos, piercings, or other modifications; and they're the same reasons we do so today. Nothing has changed in thousands of years, except the symbols themselves—and (thankfully) improved methods for doing the work!

Because we have few rites and rituals that mark life transitions or prove our devotion to a particular group or idea, body art often fills that void. Whether to signal a life passage or to enforce a belief, the ritual and permanency of body art fulfills some basic need we have as sentient beings.

Many people today get body art to mark transitions in their lives—such as turning eighteen, a death in the family, or surviving an illness or accident. These same rites of passage were once big events in which the entire community participated. Their importance was clear because of the rituals and ceremonies connected to them. Since we don't have those rituals anymore, many people find the permanency of a tattoo or other body modification a good way to mark a life-changing occasion.

Tattoos can also show allegiance to a group or philosophy. Many people, the world over, get inked to exhibit their religious convictions. Christian iconography is a typical tattoo motif; praying hands, Christ on the cross, and the Virgin Mary are images commonly made into tattoos. Skin art can also show the world other alliances you may have. Military personnel, college fraternities, members of Alcoholics Anonymous, and Deadheads all have tattoo imagery particular to their affiliations.

Others get inked for mystical reasons. It can be something simple, like a lucky number or animal; or more complex, like an entire Tibetan prayer or ancient runic symbols. These tattoos act as protective and empowering talismans for the wearer. There are even some body artists who perform ritual tattoos, piercings, brandings, and cuttings. They may suggest you consult your astrological chart to pick the right time to get your body art. They will burn incense, light candles, and let your loved ones be present, all to create a more ritualistic environment. By incorporating your personal beliefs into the process, you can make getting tattooed or pierced a truly powerful experience.

Body art is also a way of recognizing our physical bodies, celebrating our corporeal selves with marks that are aesthetically pleasing. Tattoos can really complement the body, enhancing the good parts and camouflaging the bad parts. The glint of metal jewelry against the skin is an exotic and erotic complement. There's nothing wrong with getting body art just because you think it looks good!

These days, piercing is trendy enough that people get holes in their nipples, tongues, navels, and genitals simply for style reasons, but, of course, the *real* purpose of those piercings is to increase sexual stimulation. C'mon, do you really think someone would have a twelve-gauge post inserted through a sensitive body part if there wasn't a *big* payoff? Body art makes you very conscious of your physical self—whether it's the stimulation that having a piece of metal shoved through your skin gives or just the personal satisfaction that comes from seeing your skin decorated with beautiful designs.

There are people whose body-art practices stem from an interest in the ways other contemporary cultures adorn themselves, express their beliefs, show their status, and mark important moments in their lives with tattoos, pierces, and other permanent marks. Such people are called *neotribalists*.

As the world becomes more of a "melting pot," linking us all together through advances in communication, travel, and trade, thousands of cultures are being swallowed by global Westernization. Traditions that have endured for centuries are suddenly rejected by people brainwashed into believing that television, fast food, and sneakers are more important than the values of their ancestors. Neotribalists try to preserve the unique flavor of each little pocket of civilization. They want to experience and learn from other customs, present and past, and develop their own meaningful rituals from that information.

Like many people into body art, neotribalists find the Western concept of beauty very puritanical and boring. Instead of following the clean-cut, unmarked, every-hair-in-place ideal that most Western cultures encourage, they look to the rest of the world for more variety and expressiveness in their appearance.

Modern primitives incorporate the traditions of other cultures with futuristic visions of the human race. They embrace not only the old world of magic and mystery, but the new world of cybernetics and virtual reality. They take body modification to new heights by using the latest surgical and chemical technology to re-create themselves according to their own wishes. This could mean using a piercing to create a metal "beauty mark" on your face, or implanting metal spikes under your skin that stick out of the top of your head. It also includes extreme body modifications like implanting marbles under your skin for a more reptilian look.

There is also a political element to body art. Modifying your body to what *you* want it to look like is a very strong statement. You're asserting control over your own physical being in a society that increasingly regulates what you can and can't do with it. From the moment you're born, you're bombarded with images of what your society wants you to look like. In the Western world, those images are really very plain—there's very little variety in the way we look. When you take the initiative to decorate yourself in a nontraditional manner, you're taking back power from a culture that doesn't want you to stand out or be different. You're also rejecting the conventional rules of decorum. It's *your* body and you can do what you like with it.

Of course, there's nothing wrong with getting work simply because you like the way it looks. Lots of folks find that a tattoo that follows the contours of their body can make them look thinner, shapelier, or more toned. A well-placed pierce can enhance a cute body part or camouflage a flawed one. Body art is also a good way to cover scars, birthmarks, stretch marks, and blemishes. And let's not forget the cool factor.

Since body art is still not mainstream, having marks on your body that you put there on purpose shows the world your rebellious or unconventional nature. Just make sure you're not a rebel without a clue. Don't slap ink and metal in your body to get even with your parents or try to gain instant credibility—people who do so are missing the whole point (and if you don't know what that point is by now . . .).

Once you start getting tattooed or pierced, you may find it hard to stop. You can really become addicted. It's hard to explain, but there's something about the anticipation of getting the work, the "endorphin rush" while the work is being done, and the thrill of showing off your new piece—it's a feeling like no other in the world. I promise you, once you get a tattoo or piercing that you've thought long and hard about and that has real meaning for you, you'll *never* feel the same again! It's very empowering to look at your body art and be reminded of why you did it and what it represents. It's a little part of your personality transformed into art. Besides, it just makes life on this planet more interesting, don't you think?

Whether you're getting work to mark an important moment or just covering up a birthmark, the challenge is to find something that's meaningful to you. You want to be proud of your body art and happy with it forever—so think before you ink! Make sure your tattoo is something that expresses your personality, a signature of your soul.

Below are a few personal accounts of different people's body art and their meaning.

Dennis

While in the military, Dennis and a few other soldiers in his barracks all got homemade tats from another private who had rigged up a crude tattoo machine with a small motor, a ballpoint-pen casing, and some guitar string. Dennis didn't think too

32

much about what he wanted then—the point was just to get one, since everyone else was. For years he hated the tattoo on his arm—not because of what it represented, but because of how poorly it was done. In 1995, Dennis went to a famous tattooist who specialized in Black and Gray tats in the Jailhouse tradition. Although he didn't want the original tat covered over, he did get it touched up and then had some beautiful, wispy smoke and the words *For My Bros, Ft. Jack* written around the tattoo in elegant script. This way, he kept the original meaning of the piece while turning it into a tribute to his buddies—as well as a good tattoo!

Sarah

Sarah sports a Celtic legband with a grapevine running through it. This is a representation of her heritage: her mother is Irish and her father's family worked the vineyards in Italy. She's currently designing a band for her other leg, a music staff (she's a musician) with different fruits and vegetables as the notes (she's a vegetarian). The notes correspond to the first two bars of her favorite childhood lullaby!

Jack

As a teenager, Jack pierced his ear with a needle and cork and wore one of his sister's earrings in the hole. When his father saw it, Jack was severely reprimanded. The sharpness of his father's reaction caused Jack to leave home. He didn't speak to his father for four years after that. These days, Jack sports ten holes in each ear and lobes stretched out about half an inch. While you might think that his pierc-ings are a reaction to his quarrel with his father, Jack says he's just fulfilling a desire he's had since that day with the needle and cork. He called his father two years ago and they quickly made up. They agreed to meet and Jack took wicked pleasure in his father's shocked face when he saw all of that metal in Jack's ears. "But you know what," says Jack. "He never said one word about it and he never has since."

Shelley

In the course of eighteen months, Shelley was mugged, involved in two accidents, and fell and broke her leg. She was really having a streak of bad luck and wanted to do something to break the cycle. Since she collects anything with angels, she picked her favorite angel design and got it tattooed on her shoulder. "I really felt like I needed an angel look-ing over my shoulder," she said. "I haven't had any trouble since then."

Maria

This is a girl who just loves the art of tattoo. She's a tattooist herself, her husband's a tattooist, and their house and studio are covered with tattoo memora-bilia. All of Maria's tattoos are in the Traditional style—hearts, swallows, hula girls, panthers—and they are all over her body! She's into hunting down antique flash designs and having them inked on her body. Maria takes her inspiration from the tattooed ladies of the early-twentieth-century sideshows.

Malik

Malik has one small dot tattooed on the palm of his hand. Not much of a tattoo but very special to him because mixed in with the ink used to create it is a little ash taken from the urn that holds the remains of his grandfather.

Karen

After Karen had a hysterectomy, she was self-conscious about wearing a bikini because of the big horizontal scar running along her abdomen. Even though she's not, as she put it, the "tattoo type," she had a beautiful line of flowers inked over the scar to camouflage it. She's very happy with the results and is now considering more work.

Doug

The day he turned eighteen, Doug went to the closest tattoo shop and had a big American Indian portrait tattooed on his chest. He was very proud of it and spent most of the next year shirtless, showing off his tat. It gave him confidence and that certain outlook on life tattooed people have—call it "tattitude." Soon he bought a motorcycle, dropped out of college, and headed out on the road. He spent the next twenty years traveling the U.S., stopping at any place that looked interesting for a year or so and then hitting the highway again. At each new stop, he'd add to his ink collection. Now fifty-six, he's pretty much covered with pieces large and small and considers his tattooed body a living scrapbook of his life and times. He's never regretted the direction he chose in life nor any of his skin-art mementos.

Kai

In school, she was a Girl Scout. She tutored children with learning disabilities on the weekends and graduated from high school with high honors. In college, she excelled and upon graduation landed a high-profile job in the financial world. If you saw her on the street, she would look like any corporate type, in conservative clothes and sensible shoes. But Kai has a secret. Under her navy-blue suit she sports many sexy piercings. She says she enjoys the metal in her body not just for the pleasure it gives her and her boyfriend, but because it's a way to express her wild side while protecting her professional image.

Stevie

Stevie has a strange patch of thick hair growing on his right shoulder. Although everyone else thinks it's disgusting, he's pretty attached to the black, curly growth. A while back, Stevie decided to make this oddity a little easier on other people's eyes, so he had a head tattooed under the patch of hair. Now instead of being totally repulsed, everyone gets a good chuckle.

There is no one right reason for choosing to have body art, since it's all about expressing your personality. The important thing is to take your time in deciding what you want and where you want it. When your work has been planned out, from idea to execution, you end up with living art that will bring you pleasure for a lifetime.

CHAPTER 4

LEARNING THE
LANGUAGE

HERE ARE THREE SHORT glossaries that will familiarize you
with tattoo symbolism, tattoo styles, and piercing terminology. They are by no means complete, but they will provide
you with some basics and maybe motivate you to study the
endlessly fascinating world of body art further.

TATTOO SYMBOLISM

When trying to decide what kind of tattoo you want, it's a
good idea to turn to humankind's rich tradition of symbolism. Much imagery has a legacy of meaning that dates back to
the beginning of time, culled from myths, fables, hieroglyphs,
religions, and social customs.

Symbolism is the language of the psyche and tattoos are
an expression of a person's individual consciousness. What
follows are some common tattoo images and a brief descrip-
tion of their symbolical history.

Anchor

Anchors represent security or safety. For seafaring societies,
the anchor was a mystical symbol that could prevent a ship

from sinking. To early Christians, an anchor signified salvation; like another water symbol, the fish, it represented Christ (it also bears a strong resemblance to a cross). It was frequently shown upside down, with a star, crescent, or cross indicating its spiritual nature.

Angel

In the oldest Hindu texts, angels were women who were "rewards" given to brave warriors in heaven. In alchemy, the angel represents sublimation (moving from a solid to an ethereal state), an analogy for the ability to move between earth and heaven, or the physical and spiritual states of being. In most religions, angels are heavenly beings, who are divine messengers and protectors.

Bat

In Western cultures, bats are associated with the mysterious, the unseen. Since bats use echolocation (finding an object by means of sound waves that are reflected back to who- or whatever emits them by the objects) not their eyes, to hunt and navigate, wearing a representation of a bat was thought to help a person see what's hidden. Since demons are associated with evil, they are often depicted with batlike wings. To the Chinese, bats symbolized happiness, good fortune, and longevity; to the Mayans, they were symbols of rebirth.

Bear

A ruthless and invincible foe in battle, the bear can either move on all fours or stand upright, giving it a dual nature, somewhere between animal and human. As a totem in Native American tradition, bears represented wisdom and indomitability.

Bird

All winged creatures have connotations of spirituality. Egyptians used a bird with a human head, *ba,* to express the belief that the soul flies away at death. Hindu tradition associates birds with higher states of consciousness.

Boat

As vessels by which one navigates the seas, boats have come to be associated with spiritual journeys. Boats represent the human body, waters the path of spiritual pilgrimage.

Butterfly

The ancient Greek word *psyche* means both "soul" and "butterfly." The butterfly represents the soul's ability to fly away from the body. The purification of the soul by fire is represented on ancient urns by the image of a butterfly too close to a flame. The butterfly's emergence from its cocoon is a common symbol for rebirth. Today, psychologists consider the butterfly emblematic of transformation. In China, it has the secondary meaning of joy, especially in marriage.

Cat

Across time and varying cultures, cats have been associated with witchcraft and women.

Freya, the goddess of fertility and love in Norse or Scandinavian mythology, rode in a chariot drawn by two cats. In Hindu tradition, cats are associated with the goddess of childbirth, Shasthi. Egyptians identified cats with the moon because of their nocturnal habits. They were also sacred representations of the goddess Bast, who was sometimes depicted with a cat's head. Bast presided over bountiful harvests, marriage, and fertility.

In the fifteenth century, when the agents of the Spanish Inquisition set about destroying all vestiges of ancient religions, many of which worshiped women, cats became identified as the familiars of witches and manifestations of the devil.

Clouds

Since clouds lie between heaven and earth, early Christian symbolism associates them with messages from God. The Chinese represented female sexuality in the form of clouds, giving new meaning, albeit unintentionally, to the phrase *having your head in the clouds.*

Clover

The patron saint of Ireland, Patrick, used a three-leaf clover to symbolize the Holy Trinity in Christian religion. To many ancient religions, it's a representation of the triple goddess, who has three aspects or manifestations.

The rare four-leaf clover is a representation of the mystical number four: the four seasons, the four elements, the four stages of human life, etc. Considered a symbol of luck, love, and fidelity.

Clown

In medieval courts, the jester was the inversion of the king— a buffoon, a fool. People with physical deformities are often associated with the figure of the jester. In ancient times, they were often human sacrifices. When a city suffered from a disaster, an ugly or deformed person was chosen to represent the evils that afflicted the community. These scapegoats were beaten, tortured, and burned on a pyre, a ritual performed to purge the community of its problem.

Many tattoos depict a "bad clown," an evil-looking character. This is a representation of the "trickster," a figure found in African and many other myths. The trickster is a magical being sent by the gods to vex humans. He is the great deceiver and can't be trusted or taken at face value—clowns paint a happy face over their real face.

Cobweb

Traditionally, a cobweb means the wearer has killed somebody. A representation of the fate that is "spun" for a person, its spiral shape suggests the expanding universe and the cyclical nature of life. At the beginning of the Christian era, the Gnostics depicted a spider sitting in the middle of a web to represent the belief that evil lurks not only on the "edges" of life but in the center, the very origin of existence.

Cow

A symbol of sustenance for human beings, a general representation of motherhood and nourishment. In Scandinavian mythology, the cow of Creation was Audumla, whose name meant "creator of the earth."

Cross

The most basic meaning is the joining of opposites, the horizontal and the vertical, earth and heaven, the material and spiritual, masculine and feminine. For Christians, it depicts the ultimate sacrifice—Christ's suffering on the cross.

Deer

Deer are the source of many things to people—their flesh, hide, and horns. They are great providers for human sustenance. Their horns symbolize strength and power.

Devil

The devil is a representation of worldly concerns, which stand in opposition to spiritual enlightenment. In the tarot, the devil card represents earthly desire, deviation, and confusion.

Dog

Dogs have long been thought to be keen judges of character as well as guards against unwanted intruders. In Greek mythology, a three-headed dog, Cerberus, guarded the gates of hell, just as Annubis guarded the Egyptian underworld. Protectors of the home, dogs are symbolic of loyalty and devotion.

Dolphin

Dolphins symbolize salvation, since they have a reputation as rescuers of people in the sea. According to an older symbolic meaning, they represent creation, passion, and sexuality; "dolphin" comes from the Greek word *delphinos,* which also means "womb." People in cultures that lived near the sea often believed that having a dolphin tattoo on their legs acted as protection against sharks.

Dragon

The dragon is a composite symbol of many cold-blooded animals that are hostile and frightening to humans, including some of humankind's early antagonists. In many myths, the dragon is the ultimate enemy, thus the modern psychological interpretation of the dragon symbol as a fear that a person must overcome on his or her path to maturity.

Dragons are also fierce guardians. In China, they are an emblem of imperial power, symbolizing the sovereign's protection of the people and victory over wickedness.

Eagle

Symbolizing the masculine, the eagle is generally associated with power and war. Characterized by its speed and ability as a predator, in traditions from Native America to ancient Rome, the eagle is a great warrior leader, powerful and wise.

The eagle is also associated with lightning, fire, and the sun—the great powers of the earth. When the eagle is shown carrying a victim, it represents the triumph of superior powers over baser instincts.

Elf

Elves can be helpful, granting wishes, doing humans' work while they sleep, guarding over children and animals. They can also be destructive, stealing people away or causing general mischief. A good representation of the uncontrollable, mystical nature of existence.

Fairy

Fairies represent the unseen, supernatural forces at work on earth, and like elves, are indicative of a belief in natural magic.

Feather

Egyptians believed that each soul would be weighed against the Plume of Maat (meaning truth), to determine how heavy with sin a person was. Thus, to be "light as a feather" meant that one was free of sin.

Feathers correlate with the element of air and the desire to break free of earthly bonds. In Native American societies, feathers are a powerful totem for spiritual enlightenment, used in rituals and as adornment.

Fire

Fire is the ultimate symbol of life, embodying both good (body heat, warmth) and bad (destruction). It's a symbol for the duality of our existence, at once an agent of death and destruction and a bringer of spiritual rebirth by purgation.

Fish

The fish was an early sign of Christianity, symbolizing the spiritual world that lies below the material world. It was chosen because fish inhabit water, a mysterious, unknown world. Because water is associated with the unformed and the subconscious, they symbolize dreams and visions.

The *vesica piscis* (vessel of the fish) was a female genital symbol that looked like a crude representation of the body of a fish. Thus fish also are a representation of the womb, or more directly, the womb's exit.

Flower

The language of flowers is complicated and intricate, with each variety and color having a specific meaning. Generally, a flower, by its very nature, represents the bounty and beauty of spring. The flower is an image of the natural unfolding of life.

Frog

Because of frogs' amphibian nature, able to hop between water (the original mother-womb) and land (our earthly home), they represent fertility and birth.

Gargoyles

Gargoyles, in their fiendish appearance, are designed to keep evil away. In the Middle Ages, cathedrals were covered with gargoyles to protect their sanctity. In the hierarchy of architectural ornamentation, gargoyles are always placed under angels and other enlightened beings.

Heart

The heart has always been considered the center, a symbol of the eternal soul. Because a person's center represents his soul, the heart also represented the magnetic attraction one person has for another. To love is to encounter an overwhelming force that urges a lover toward his beloved's center. In Christian iconography, the heart is often pictured with flames, a cross, or a crown to represent spiritual love.

Knife

The symbolical opposite of the sword, which has a lofty spiritual meaning, the knife is analogous to the phallus and the masculine instincts of vengeance and combat. The short blade of the knife represents the physical strength of the person wielding it, whereas the long blade of the sword depicts the spiritual justness of the person.

Lion

The Roman sun god, Mithras, was represented in leonine form. The cult of Mithras was restricted to men, predominantly military men, so the lion has always been associated with brute strength, power, and other masculine traits. In African ritual dances, men became lions, harnessing their abilities for use in battle. The lion is king of the jungle, the earthly opposite of the ruler of the sky, the eagle.

Mandala

A ritualistic, geometric design. A symbolical "map" of the universe, used as a meditational tool in Hinduism and Buddhism. A mandala is a visual aid in the contemplation of the complexity of life.

Mermaid

Mermaids spring from the tradition of water goddesses, who are associated with the womb (see *Fish*). In Africa, the goddess Yemaya was depicted with seaweed for hair and shells for jewelry. In India, the Nagas were human above the waist and water snakes below.

Mermaids that lure seafarers to their death can be found in many cultures' folklore. In this sense, they can be equated with the temptations one encounters "navigating" the course of one's life.

When you regard the sea as a representation of the subconscious, a half-human/half-fishlike creature symbolizes the two aspects of human consciousness, the subliminal and the sentient.

Moon —

The moon's movements are cyclical in nature. Its changing shape corresponds to the stages of life.

The lunar cycle influences the physiological cycle of a woman, as well as the tides of the ocean—deep, mysterious events. The moon is associated with the feminine, and with moon goddesses such as Ishtar, Diana, and Artemis.

Because of its close association with the mysteries of the night and the hidden, subconscious quality of water, the moon is associated with imagination, mystery, and magic.

The moon tarot card illustrates the mysteries of the world. The "lunar way" is feminine, relying on intuition and magic; the "solar way" is masculine, relying on reason and objectivity.

Octopus

The octopus is related to the center of Creation, a specific core with tentacles reaching outward. As a creature of the sea, it's associated with the subconscious and unknown forces.

Panther

Known for their aggressiveness and strength, these large cats are also night hunters, which adds mystery to their activities. They are associated with the Roman Dionysus and the Greek Bacchus, the god of wine, revelry, and fertility. Mix all of the aforementioned qualities together and you have a masculine totem that gives you power through occult and sexual ability.

Rose

Because of its shape and nature, it's associated with the vagina. Like all flowers, it symbolizes beauty and perfection. Deeper meanings are derived from the color and number of petals. It was a sacred symbol of the Roman goddess of sexual love and physical beauty, Venus.

Sacred Heart

The Catholic saint Margaret Marie Alacoque had a vision in which her heart was surrounded by a crown of thorns, representing Christ. This is the source of the symbol.

Serpent/Snake

The characteristics of the snake explain some of its symbolic significance. Because it sheds its skin and is "reborn," it represents immortality. Because of its quick, serpentine movements, it represents strength. Because of its vicious nature, it represents evil and treachery in the natural world. Because of its shape, it represents the phallus.

From Native American ritual to Greek mythology and ancient Sumerian theology, the snake is a symbol of healing through transformation.

Shark

In the language of the Haida, a Native American people inhabiting Canada and Alaska whose art has been borrowed by a popular tattoo style, the word *shark* means the "dogfish mother"—the womb that bites. It is the sharp-toothed "mouth" that is ancient and deadly enough to deserve our utmost respect.

Skeleton

The ultimate symbol of death. When a skeleton is depicted in a lifelike stance, it represents life after death. The skulls of an enemy were often kept by the victors. In many cultures, wearing the skull as a totem indicates the wearer has no fear of death.

Smoke

Smoke corresponds to the powerful spiritual elements of air and fire. Many religions used smoke in rituals meant to ward off evil. Smoke is symbolic of the transition from earth to heaven, indicating the path to salvation through fire. Medieval alchemists used smoke to represent the soul leaving the body.

Spider

The spider as a symbol has three distinct determinations: creativity is symbolized by the spider weaving its web; infinity is represented by the figure-eight shape of the spider's body;

and chaos is represented by the spider's pattern of building and destroying webs, luring prey then killing them.

In Indian tradition, the spider in its web is representative of "maya," a concept of the mysterious, incomprehensible nature of the world. Maya is the eternal weaving of the web of illusion—or the world as we see it, not as it really is.

Star

The ancients considered stars to be souls in the sky. They are also identified with ancient fertility goddesses like Astarte and Ishtar.

As a light that shines in the night, a star represents the spirit struggling against the forces of darkness. For seafaring people, who used them as navigational tools, stars were guideposts from heaven.

Special stars in the sky have always symbolized the imminent coming of a prophet or savior, as in the birth of Christ.

The hexagram, or six-pointed star, is an ancient good-luck symbol called the Seal of Solomon. In the nineteenth century, it became a universal symbol for Jews, corresponding to the Christian cross. It's called the Star of David because of the belief that a hexagram was pictured on the first King of Israel's shield. Before that, the hexagram was used in India to symbolize sexual union, with Kali represented by the downward-pointing triangle and Shiva represented by the upward-pointing triangle.

Egyptian hieroglyphics interpreted the five-pointed star, the pentagram or pentacle, as the spirit rising up toward its point of origin. The pentagram is formed by one continuous line and is used to ward off evil. An inverted five-pointed star is symbolic of the infernal when used in black magic.

Sun

A masculine symbol, representing ultimate power and sovereignty, the sun is personified by the Egyptian god Ra (or Re), the son of heaven. As such, he possesses the best of all attributes: he sees all and knows all. Ra is the supreme deity, represented as a man with the head of a hawk crowned with a sun disk and a sacred serpent.

Associated with heroism, courage, and spiritual illumination, the sun is the original father, the divine eye, the source of all life—the opposite creative power to the moon. The sun is unchanging and eternal.

Sunflower

Since the sunflower loves the sun (the ultimate symbol of masculine creation) and follows its path across the sky, it can be interpreted as feminine adoration for the male and his reproductive capabilities.

Sword

Like the cross, the sword is a symbol of the phallus and has always been the property of men, a tool of war and defense. In medieval lore, a sword is the instrument by which a knight defends the forces of light against the forces of dark—symbolical of a hero's spiritual courage. A sword depicted with fire or flames represents purification through a quest.

Tiger

The tiger is associated with wrath and cruelty, the superior hunter with no mercy for its prey. Chinese philosophy equates the tiger with darkness and the new moon (darkness always implies darkness of the soul).

A Chinese symbol of five different-colored tigers represents the order of space and the elements against the forces of inconceivable chaos (the Chinese have five elements, not four). According to this concept, the Red Tiger reigns in the south; his season is summer, his element fire. The Black Tiger governs in the north; his season is winter and his element water. The Blue Tiger's domain is the east, in the spring and among vegetation. The White Tiger dominates the west, in autumn and among the metals. The Yellow Tiger inhabits all the earth and rules supreme.

Unicorn

The unicorn is a phallic symbol, its single horn being its most prominent and unique feature. The oldest legends of the unicorn describe it as a very swift horse with a single horn, who doesn't like humans and is almost impossible to catch. The only way to snare a unicorn is to lure it with a virgin, whose very presence will cause the animal to fall submissively at her feet. For this reason, the unicorn is associated with purity and innocence.

Water

In the oldest Hindu sacred texts, the Vedas, water is referred to as *mâtriamâh* ("the most maternal") because it is the beginning of all life. Water is Mother, the beginning of all things. The enduring nature of water suggests infinity; the vigorous nature of water suggests movement and transition. Because of its mysterious, dark nature, it is often associated with the subconscious.

Baptism predates Christianity and was representative of transformation, protection from evil, and immortality. Baptism in water, as practiced by Christians, is the symbolic death of the sinner, who emerges reborn to salvation.

Waves

Waves signify infinity, as suggested by the endless repetiveness of their movement.

Whale

The original Jonah and the Whale story can be traced all the way back to Babylonia and the sea goddess called the Whale of Det (Derceto), who swallowed the god Oannes and then "gave birth" to him. The Polynesian warrior Nganaoa was also swallowed by a monstrous sea creature and then returned to the world, as was the Finnish warrior Ilmainen. Being devoured by a whale indicates a rite of passage through which one is transformed. As with other creatures of the sea, the whale symbolizes a spiritual womb.

Wolf

Fenris, a wolf in Nordic mythology, was said to be held in shackles in the bowels of the earth. He would break free at the world's end to devour the sun, thus ending all life. In pre-Christian Europe, many tribes had wolf rituals during which men "became" wolves. Typified by their predatory skills and night prowling, they are mysterious and dangerous creatures and represent the dark, destructive side of man.

TATTOO STYLES

New styles and hybrid styles of tattoo design are coming into existence every day. As the visual language and tastes of our culture change, so does the language of tattoos. Here are some basics to help you identify what you see and articulate what you want.

Black and Gray

Work done only with black ink or dye (and the resulting shades of gray), is put in the skin with a single needle. The technique is also called *Joint Style* or *Jailhouse* because it origi-

nated in penitentiaries. Prisoners would handmake tattoo machines that were electrically powered by small, available motors (like the ones found in tape players). Their pigments were also handmade from, among other things, cigarette ashes and pen ink, and there was little variety besides shades of black.

The Jailhouse style was adapted and expanded by tattooists in the late 1970s and early 1980s and renamed Black and Gray. It's customarily used for portraiture or realistic pieces, since the artist focuses on the line and shading of the piece. As with other Fine Line work, the tattooist must be careful not to put too much detail into too small an area.

Biomechanical

Inspired by the "part human/part machine" artistic musings of people like Clive Barker and H. R. Giger, Biomechanical tattoos are often *trompe l'oeil*—i.e., they give the illusion that the wearer's skin has been peeled back to reveal steel rods and computer boards instead of muscles and bones—picture the Bionic Man with updated technology. Other pieces combine organic and artificial subject matter into an eerie hybrid. The ultimate cyberpunk skin art.

Celtic

Celtic designs often represent people and animals from Welsh, Breton, Gaelic, and Cornish folklore; they incorporate intricate weavings of a single line, called *knotwork*. Many Celtic designs originate from a famous tome created by monks in the sixth century called *The Book of Kells*. This book combined the ancient pagan religion of Central and Western Europe with Anglo-Roman Christian traditions in ornate illustrations. The original book can now be found at Trinity College in Dublin.

Darkside

Death and darkness have always been a classic tattoo theme—skulls, snakes, demons, spiders, and spiderwebs are all conventional tattoo imagery. Darkside tattooing takes our fascination with mortality, death, isolation, fear, and evil to new levels. Inspired by fantasy/sci-fi/horror illustrations, intricate renderings of ghouls, ghosts, demons, mummies, vampires, and scenes of debauchery and heresy give the wearer a dangerous aura. There's a heavy emphasis on smooth shading and fine detail, and the best examples of this work have great depth and dimension.

Fantasy

Fantasy tattoos run the gamut from unicorns and wizards to intricate scenes of medieval battles and mythical characters. They are generally rendered in an array of colors to convey the fantastical elements of the work.

Gangster

The idea of Gangster tattoos comes from the habit of gang members tattooing the name or symbol of their crew on their

bodies to signify permanent allegiance, very much in the ancient tradition of tribal identification. Usually this takes the form of having your crew's name or motto tattooed in some kind of script on your stomach or back. There are also complex tattoo languages used in Gangster tattoos; for example, "cholo tears" are teardrops tattooed around your eyes, each drop representing someone the wearer killed.

Haida

The simple but expressive artwork of this Native American tribe (from the Queen Charlotte Islands of Canada and Prince of Wales Island in Alaska) has given rise to many popular tattoo motifs. Many people sport Haida renderings of animals or abstract designs. These are generally done in flat black, with red or another color as a highlight. (See page 59.)

Memorial

Memento mori, or "In Memory Of . . .", tattoos are usually a portrait of the person with his name, birth, and death dates. Memorial tattoos can also signify the birth of a child or a wedding.

New School

New School tattooing incorporates other skin-art styles (Western Traditional, Oriental, Fine Line) with fine-art and folk-art traditions to make a "multiculti" tattoo stew. New Schoolers often use subject matter that was previously considered inappropriate for tattoos, and radical styles from kitsch to cubism, to turn out big, beautiful works of skin art. Their color palette is bounteous, with hues that push the boundaries of pigment possibilities.

New School was born out of the fresh approach toward tattooing that developed in the early 1980s, when the scene was discovered by fine artists and exploded out of the underground. These eager young artists infused new vigor, creativity, and openness into a craft that was usually done in the "old days" (twenty years ago) in secrecy and with great mistrust. Prior to this new breed of tattooists, who treated the form more like an art than a craft, most tattooists hoarded technical information like Houdini hoarded his tricks, for fear of losing business to some young gun with a steadier hand. They also did little to expand the range of conventional tattoo imagery. That's commonly known as "old-school attitude." New School signifies a revolution not only in style and technique, but in spirit. So even more than a method, it's a philosophy.

Oriental

Oriental-style tattooing usually refers to traditional Japanese tattooing. Colorful and intricate, concerned with musculature and placement, using a limited vocabulary of design motifs—fish,

water, lotus flowers, religious imagery—Oriental style also implies that the work covers the whole physique. There's no such thing as a small Oriental piece. A person's work is planned out to cover the entire body, every inch of skin to be tattooed is mapped out and accounted for before the work begins. For centuries in Japan, tattooing, or *irezumi,* indicated that you were *yakuza* (a Japanese gangster) and was therefore associated with the criminal class, much as tattooed people in the West are.

Tribal

Along with Traditional, this is one of the most confusing tattoo terms around. Just what tribe are we referring to? Tattoos can be traced back thousands of years and are found the world over. What we think of as Tribal tattoos are generally black, abstract tattoos, based on designs found in Polynesia, Micronesia, and Borneo. Tribal can either be based on geometric patterns or organic lines that fit a person's body perfectly.

Wild Style

Based on hip-hop culture and skateboard and graffiti art, Wild Style runs the gamut—it can be a "tag" spray-painted on your body or a killer board design.

GLOSSARY OF PIERCING TERMINOLOGY

Ampallang

A male piercing done horizontally through the head of the penis, sometimes placed above the urethra (the passage that carries urine and semen out of a man's body), sometimes going through the urethra.

Antitragus

A piercing of the ear through the cartilage opposite the tragus.

Apadravya

Same type of procedure as the ampallang, but here the barbell enters vertically through the penis head and exits at its base.

The apadravya provides increased sexual sensitivity for the wearer and his partner.

Autoclave

A pressurized container used for sterilization. Every piercer or tattooist *must* have one of these and they must have it checked on a regular basis. All tools used in piercing and tattooing have to be autoclaved after each use. This is the only suitable method for destroying pathogenic bacterium, which cause infection and disease.

Barbell

A common body-jewelry design, recognizable as a long post with beads that screw into one or both ends. Barbells can be straight, curved, or horseshoe-shaped; the placement of your piercing will determine which barbell you need.

Beauty spot or beauty mark

Also called a Chrome Crawford (à la Cindy Crawford's famous beauty mark), this piercing uses a stud with a bead on one end, above the upper lip, slightly off to the side.

Bridge

A piercing done between the eyes on the bridge of the nose. This is a difficult pierce and one that does not easily heal.

Caliper

An instrument used to measure thickness and distances in piercing.

Cheek

A risky piercing because of the potential damage to nerves and blood vessels. It requires two lengths of labret studs, an initial longer length, and a shorter one once the swelling has subsided.

Clit or clitoris

The clitoris is pierced at the base, either vertically or horizontally. Most women prefer a captive ring for jewelry because the bead acts as a sexual stimulator.

Clit hood or hood

The flap of skin that covers the clitoris is also a popular spot for a sexually enhancing piercing. The trick is to properly place the piercing so that when a women is sexually excited, the bead of the clit-hood piercing lies directly on the clitoris, providing additional stimulation. Can be done vertically or horizontally.

Conch or concha

An ear piercing done in the recessed part of the ear leading to the ear canal.

Daith or daitch

This is an ear piercing that is done in the cartilage that curves into the inner part of the ear, above the tragus. A popular piercing, it can be very subtle with a small ring or really noticeable with bigger jewelry.

Diameter

One of the two measurements pertinent to body jewelry. The diameter is the measured space inside a ring or curved barbell, which corresponds to the length of barbells.

It's important to get jewelry wide enough or long enough to allow for swelling that may occur after the initial piercing. Once the swelling disappears, you can get a smaller piece of jewelry.

Downsizing

A term used when a pierce requires an initial jewelry size and then a smaller one after the swelling has gone down and it has sufficiently healed.

Dydoes

A penis piercing that should only be done on circumcised men. Dydoes are a pair of barbells placed on either side of the coronal rim of the penis head (if you're uncircumcised, this rim is covered by the foreskin unless the penis is erect). This piercing is another sexual enhancement, rumored to have been created by a Jewish medical student who wanted to re-place some of the sensation he felt he'd lost by being circum-cised.

Earlets or eyelets

A kind of jewelry used to show off stretched holes in your ears or nose. These hollow tubes have flanged ends to keep them in place. They look great by themselves, because you can see clearly through the hollow center, or you can hang other pieces of jewelry through them. Also known as "flesh tunnels."

Earlobe

The world's most common piercing is done on the soft, fleshy, lower part of the external ear.

Ear Project (a.k.a. Industrial)

Two or more piercings through which a single piece of jewelry is worn. This kind of piercing art requires planning. The piercer must initially measure the holes that will be threaded with one piece of jewelry, then put separate jewelry in each hole. After the holes have sufficiently healed, another piece of jewelry can be threaded through the holes to create a "woven" effect.

Eyebrow

As a rule, these piercings loop the eyebrow (if you're wearing a ring) or have one bead sticking out of the top and one out of the bottom (if you're wearing a barbell).

Forceps

An instrument that looks like a pair of tongs, used for grabbing and pulling a few layers of skin away from the rest of the derma.

Frenum

A layer of tissue that holds an organ in place, like the flap that connects the underside of the tongue to the floor of the mouth. As a piercing, it's commonly done on the underside of the penis, below the head. Barbell studs are the most common piece of jewelry used. Placement of this piercing is crucial so that the wearer doesn't experience discomfort when sitting. For a more unique piercing, the membrane under the tongue (called a frenulum) can be pierced, and a small ring placed in the hole.

Gauge

Measurement that identifies how thick a piece of body jewelry is. The lowest gauge number, 00, is the thickest piece of jewelry. Gauge, along with diameter, are the two sizing entities involved in body piercing.

Gauge wheel

An instrument used to measure jewelry.

Guiche

This male piercing is placed through the skin found between the anus and scrotum sac. Gentlemen rave about the sensation of having their guiche ring rhythmically hit the back of their testes while they walk or run.

Hafada

A male piercing done on the scrotum sac to increase sensation.

Helix

A piercing done on the folded rim of skin and cartilage around most of the outer ear.

Labia

Both the outer and inner labia can be pierced. Originally, these piercings were used as a chastity measure, with some sort of barrier device threaded through the piercings to prevent intercourse. These days, the whole purpose of labia piercings is to increase female sexual stimulation. Labia piercings are done with rings or circular barbells. As with a frenum piercing on a man, placement must be carefully determined, otherwise the wearer will experience discomfort when sitting.

Insertion taper

The insertion taper has a fine point on one end and gradually flares out; it's used to reopen or stretch existing piercings.

Keloid

This is a fibrous scar your body makes when trying to do extreme tissue repair because of a puncture, wound, or surgical incision. Sometimes in piercings, people get hard, knotty growths around the hole. That's keloid scarring.

Labret

A popular piercing done in the area below the lip and above the chin. It requires a special labret stud: a barbell with one flat end (to lie flush against the inside of your mouth) and one screw-on end. After it's healed, some people insert rings that loop through their lower lips; others prefer the aggressive look of a spike sticking out of their labret pierces.

Latex gloves

Latex gloves are one of the ways professional piercers (or tattooists) protect against spreading infection and disease. Every piercer *must* wear latex gloves when touching sterilized tools or jewelry, as well as while performing a piercing or touching a fresh piercing. Gloves must be changed if the wearer accidentally touches something that is not sterile (like a telephone, money, etc.). No glove, no pierce!

Migrate

This refers to a piercing slowly moving from its original spot, which is caused by jewelry that's too thin. Think of people who have worn thin, wire earrings in their pierced ears for many years. The original holes have slowly moved down their lobes, leaving a noticeable slash in their wake.

Mouth

The mouth can be pierced anywhere around the lips, as well as above, below, or to the side. Whether you have a bead ring hanging off the side of your mouth or a cute little "beauty spot" stud above your lip, this is a versatile area. There are also places inside the mouth that can be pierced, like the frenulum and tongue. The only drawback to any mouth piercing is that this is an area that tends to swell a lot, so many of these piercings may require two jewelry sizes, one for the initial piercing and one for when the swelling goes down.

Lorum

A variation of the male frenum piercing, done at the spot where the base of the penis joins the scrotum sac.

Navel

A favorite of supermodels and disco divas, it's also a tricky area to pierce. The size and shape of the jewelry, the properties of the navel (innie or outie, plenty of flesh surrounding the area or super-thin), and even the nature of the body of the person having the work done all play a role in a successful navel piercing. Far too many inexperienced piercers "do navels" on people without any consideration for the above factors. This is one reason why navels have the highest rate of rejection and/or infection among common piercings. The piercer must know what any particular body can withstand as far as depth of piercing and gauge/weight of jewelry.

Also, because of the location of the navel, it's easy to irritate the new piercing, which can lead to improper healing. The navel can also be subject to fungal infections—a yeasty, cottage-cheese-like discharge. Finally, there are very strict aftercare procedures with this piercing. Many people do not properly care for their navels and that's why you see a lot of infections.

Niobium

A metal commonly used for body jewelry. It's extremely hypoallergenic and safe for most people's initial piercings. Through the process of anodization (using electrical currents and oxides to coat a metallic surface), niobium is produced in a variety of colors. It is lightweight and noncorrosive, but the color can come off from constant handling.

Nipples

A popular and pleasurable piercing for both women and men. All kinds of jewelry can be worn in nipple piercings (and hung off them!). The important rule of thumb is that the piercing must be made through the center of the nipple. This is another pierce that can be a little tricky to heal and it's imperative that you follow the aftercare instructions!

Nostril

This piercing normally takes either a ring or a nostril screw (the post is spiraled to keep the jewelry from falling out). The nostril can swell a lot when initially pierced, so be prepared.

Plug

A cylindrical, solid piece of jewelry that's held in place by a rubber ring on each end. Used in stretched piercings.

Prince Albert

The story is that this piercing was worn by Queen Victoria of England's husband, Prince Albert himself, to prevent any unseemly erections from popping up when he was in the presence of his wife. This piercing goes through the urethra and generally exits through the area where the shaft and the head meet. Traditionally, a ring is worn (through which the prince threaded a piece of leather to bind his penis to his leg) or a curved barbell.

Reject

The art of piercing is "tricking" the body into accepting a foreign object that it naturally wants to reject. This is done by piercing with the proper depth, width, and diameter, using the appropriate tools, jewelry, and procedures. When the above favorable conditions aren't met, the jewelry will force its way out.

Rook

The top ridge of cartilage on the upper ear. A good place for rings.

Scrumper

A piercing of the upper- or lower-lip frenum. A ring encircles the lip.

Septum

A thin partition that divides two cavities or soft masses of tissue in an organism, in this case, the nostrils. Just about anything goes with this piercing, from bead rings to wooden tusks. This is one procedure where piercers must really know their stuff and where you must be very careful to keep this hole from getting infected, since this area shares a common blood supply with the brain.

Septum retainer

A horseshoe-shaped piece of jewelry placed through a septum piercing. The two ends are then tucked up into the nostrils so that the piercing can't be seen. Used to keep a hole open when you're not wearing jewelry.

Surface-to-surface

Rather than completely going through tissue or cartilage (like nipples or ears), this piercing enters and exits through a few layers of skin so that the piercing "sits" on the surface of your body. Piercers must have a very good knowledge of anatomy and dermatology so that they don't go too deeply or not deeply enough. Some surface-to-surface piercings are made through the nape of the neck, the web of skin between the thumb and forefinger, or the top side of a finger, where a ring would normally be worn. These are very hard piercings to keep; they're easily snagged and ripped out of your skin. It's probably best to consider them temporary piercings; wear them for a little while, and then take the jewelry out and let the holes heal.

Stud

Another term for a barbell post.

Surgical stainless steel

A metal commonly used for body jewelry. Surgical stainless steel should be of the highest grade, 316-L, the same grade used for implants in the body. It's extremely nonreactive, it doesn't tarnish, it's scratch-resistant and very strong, so it won't bend.

Temporary piercing

Many people are getting into nonpermanent piercings, which are done just for the moment (whether that's an hour, a day, a month, or longer). They're usually done with very large gauges (which means small holes), such as a twenty or eighteen, so that when the jewelry is removed, there will be little or no scarring.

Titanium

Another metal commonly used for body jewelry. It's extremely hypoallergenic and safe for most people's initial piercings. Through the process of anodization (using electrical currents and oxides to coat a metallic surface), titanium is produced in a variety of colors. It is lightweight and noncorrosive, but bodily fluids like urine and sweat can wear away the color over time.

Tongue

The tongue can be pierced almost anywhere along its center. Placement of the piercing and size of the jewelry is important because you don't want your speech affected—some people sound like they have marbles in their mouths after they get their tongues pierced! The pierce is done with a barbell and requires downsizing. Because the tongue is a very muscular organ that gets a lot of use, it's important that the barbell be large enough so that it doesn't get pulled into the piercing by the reflexive action of the tongue.

Tragus

A flap of cartilage in front of the opening of the ear, located where your jaw is jointed together. This piercing can take many different kinds of jewelry.

CHAPTER 5

GETTING
GOOD WORK

THE KEY TO ASSURING a great piece of permanent body art is planning your work, whether tattoos or piercing. The more knowledgeable you are about the process—from concept through exceution—the better your work will be and the happier you'll be with it.

Also think about adding on to your existing work in the future. Some people have a bunch of little tattoos on their arm—and that's what it looks like: a bunch of little tattoos on their arm—they don't "tie in." Others get ten or twelve holes in their ear and then are unable to do anything more creative, like stretching. If you are seriously considering a lot of body work, you must deliberate about each piece and consider the end result. This is your only body and the work is permanent—make it a beautiful expression of your own creativity.

SUCCESSFUL SKIN ART

In order to get a good tattoo, you have to know what you want. This is a permanent decision, so don't be impulsive and *just pick something*. You may think the cover of that Melvins CD is the coolest piece of artwork you've ever seen, but who knows how you'll feel about that illustration or the Melvins in another year? Part of the fun and a lot of the reward of having a tattoo is the research process. Do your homework and don't rush into anything.

"Homework" is thinking long and hard about what you want permanently etched in your body. Don't get the tattoo your friends, lovers, or family members want you to get—give it a little thought: Do you really want a tattoo? What can you put on your body that will always be meaningful to you? It's important to take all the time you need to come up with just the right piece. Research the design possibilities, how you want it to look, whom you want to do it, how big you want it, and where you want it. If you thoroughly research and plan out your work, you'll know when you've hit on the right combination.

Don't try to price-shop for a tattoo. There's a common saying among ink slingers: *Good work is not cheap and cheap work is not good.* Save up until you can afford the tattoo you want, or make several appointments so that you pay as you go, or wait. If you really *must* have some ink and you have little cash, start with a small, more affordable piece from a great tattooist, instead of a big, terrible piece from someone who'll do whatever you want for whatever cash you have.

Some tattooists charge by the piece, some by the hour. The hourly rates usually range from fifty to a hundred dollars. Just because a tattooist doesn't charge a hundred dollars an hour doesn't mean the tattooist is no good—it depends on the location, how much in demand or well known the tattooist is, maybe even what time of year it is (more people have work done in the warm months, when their skin is exposed). There are plenty of wonderful tattooists who aren't "famous," so don't think you should only get tattooed by people you read about in magazines or see at conventions. Some ink slingers don't like all that attention. In Chapter 8, there's lots of good tips about finding a great tattooist.

Beware of scratchers. Scratchers are people who tattoo although they have no skill in the art. Often they've purchased their equipment and supplies out of a mail-order catalog and just set up shop without doing an apprenticeship or even practicing a lot. They don't have control of their tattoo machines, so they often dig too deeply, causing scarring, or they don't "hit" deep enough, leaving patchy, uneven work that looks terrible and won't last long. Their lines are uneven, unconnected, or "blown out." Scratchers will promise you the sun and the moon but have no good examples of their work to back it up. If their work looks bad in pictures or on other people, then it's just bad work, no matter what excuse they offer. A scratcher will offer to do a full back piece for an outrageously low price—and when you see the outcome, you'll know why!

What are the elements of a good tattoo? There are four main considerations in getting a great piece of ink. *Concept:* what you want to get. *Design:* how that concept is translated into a tattoo. *Placement:* where you put that design. And *execution:* how the tattooist does the work.

CONCEPT

A concept is your idea for a tattoo. Ideas for tattoos can come from anywhere. They can be realistic representations of something (a person, an object, a scene), abstract (shapes, patterns, and lines), words (different kinds of calligraphy, different alphabets), or borrowings from the great mosaic of artistic and tattoo traditions (Celtic knots, Mayan heiroglyphs, Victorian wallpaper patterns)—anything that means something to you!

Start by buying tattoo magazines and books; they give you an idea of what other people have and which artists excel at certain styles. And don't be afraid to ask tattooed people about their work. What do they have? Where and why did they get it?

If you're drawn to a particular subject, like dragons, start saving all the different representations of dragons you see every day. Whether it's a photograph, a cartoon, or a logo—the more examples you have, the easier it will be for you to decide exactly how you want your dragon to look. Your tattooist can also help you find the perfect design.

Tattooists use either *flash* (predrawn designs, usually decorating the shop walls or contained in a large book) or make custom designs (you come to them with an idea or an example of what you want and they draw it up). You should have a clear idea of what you want before you make an appointment—some tattooists won't touch you if you don't know *what* you want and *why* you want it! It's not uncommon for a tattooist to ask you the reasons behind your choice. This lets the tattooist determine whether or not you're serious about the work you're about to get. No conscientious ink slinger wants to tattoo someone who hasn't given their ink a lot of thought. They understand that it's a lifetime commitment, and for many people, one of the few permanent commitments they'll ever make! They take great pride in their craft and want their work to be beautiful, enduring pieces that the wearer will always be proud to have.

Most tattoo aficionados will tell you that custom work is far superior to "off the wall" flash. Tattooists either buy flash from other sources or draw their own. Either way, it is a design that anyone can have tattooed on himself. Custom work guarantees that your tattoo is unique, that you'll never see anyone else with the same piece. Even though flash designs are considered less appealing than custom tattoos, most tattooists will alter flash designs and personalize them to make them a little different so that you don't end up with the exact same piece as a thousand other people.

DESIGN

Do you want your dragon to be realistic or impressionistic? Do you want color work or black and gray? Do you want the whole dragon or just its head? Is the dragon snarling, ready to pounce, or lying down? Is there a background behind your dragon? The more you know about what you want, the easier it will be for you to get it. Don't worry, though: the responsibility for choosing the design is not entirely on your shoulders. Your tattooist will help you figure out just what can be accomplished with your idea.

Composition is a primary consideration in any design. Composition means the tattooist takes everything you want (the dragon, the colors, the background) and translates it into a "readable" tattoo. The artist can't cram too much detail into a small space. One of the most common problems a tattooist faces is clients who want that big, detailed, colorful design shrunk down to a little two-inch piece. Let's say you want a green-and-brown dragon that has a long, scaly tail and flaring red nostrils and sharp, gray claws, with orange-and-yellow flames shooting out of his mouth—do you really think all of that visual information can be put into a two-inch space? Remember, the more complex the piece, the bigger it will have to be. Your skin is a living, changing organism. As you get older, the tattoo lines will become less defined, and the colors will fade. If you try to put too much detail or too many colors into a small area, the tattoo will blur and look like mush. A good tattooist uses a large enough area in a design so that as age and gravity do their thing, your tattoo will still be clearly visible. Having sufficient negative space will give the tattoo a little breathing room as well.

On the other hand, you don't want so much negative space that the piece isn't interesting and cohesive. The lines must be thick enough, and the detail full enough, that your tattoo doesn't look like a bunch of unconnected elements that will just fade into oblivion. If you ask for just the *outline* of a dragon, it may not look like much. It might need colors and shading and details in the scales and flames to bring it to life.

A tattooist may go through several drafts of a piece before you are both happy with the design.

PLACEMENT

Where you put your tattoo is almost as important as what you get tattooed. Placement is integral to the design process. Long, thin lines (such as a dragon's tail) look best on the long, thin parts of your body (such as your arm or your leg), and curvier lines (such as a dragon's head) look better on the rounder parts of your body (such as your biceps or pectoral muscles).

The shape, width, and length of the design correlates directly to where the tattoo should be placed. There's nothing funnier than a pumped-up two-hundred-pound muscle boy with a teeny-weeny dagger on his upper arm. It doesn't complement his round, well-defined muscles at all—it looks more like an ugly birthmark!

A good tattooist is always concerned about the "flow" of the design—how well it complements the recesses and protusions of the client's physique. Your body is not a two-dimensional canvas; your tattoo should flatter your form, look very natural and organic, and not stick out, look awkward, or obliterate your musculature.

Another placement issue is practical rather than aesthetic. A conscientious tattooist will not tattoo a first-timer on his hands, head, or neck, because it's impossible to cover these tattoos up with clothing. If you really want a tattoo in one of those places, try one out somewhere else first. See how people react to a tattoo on a less conspicuous place before you jump into those radical areas. It's a good idea for any first-timer to get a tattoo in a spot that's easily concealed, such as the upper arm, back, torso, or buttocks.

You and your friends may think it's very cool to have sleeved arms or a big leg piece, but what about potential employers or mates? You may feel like an unconventional, F-the-world rebel right now, but who's to say how you'll feel next week, next month, or next year? There'll be time to get that skull tattooed on your hand *after* you've made your first million and don't have to worry about getting turned down for jobs because of a tattoo. Of course, some people desire radical ink to reinforce their commitment to a life outside the mainstream. Use common sense to make the right decision.

EXECUTION

This is the nuts and bolts of a good piece and how to tell if a tattooist is skilled. As well as being established, well-liked, creative, or "certified" (certified by whom? The Acme Correspondence School of Tattooing?), your tattooist must be a capable draftsperson. Any tattooist who tells you they don't need to know how to draw, just how to trace, is a fool. On the other hand, anyone who draws well and thinks he can just pick up a tattoo machine and start laying in ink is a moron. Tattooing requires creativity, artistic ability, and technical skill.

Look at other pieces your tattooist has done and don't settle for so-so, kinda-sorta work. If the tattooist's work isn't artistically and technically excellent (misshapen body parts, crooked lines, spotty color) *leave!* If you settle for less-than-perfect work, you're not going to be happy.

The first thing to check out is the outline. It should be consistent in size and form—not thin, then thick, then thin again. The outline shouldn't "skip" (the line is unconnected in some places), "explode" (expand into a big blotch in the middle of a line), or cross over another line where it's not supposed to. If the tattooer is incapable of drawing a clean, regulated line, he's definitely not the artist for you—or anyone!

The next thing to notice is the tattooist's shading. Shading is a very subtle talent; the color must gradually lighten or darken. It requires a fine touch—too much or too little shading makes for a really sloppy, cheap-looking tattoo.

You must also check out the way the tattooist lays in the color. The most important thing is that the color is even. You don't want "fill-in" that looks like a bad crayon drawing. The color should be consistent all the way through, not patchy (light in one spot, dark in the other). And it should definitely stay within the lines!

Too often, the uneducated tattoo consumer wants a complicated piece done really small, placed in a bad spot, or duplicated exactly like a flat design that the tattooist knows won't read on a three-dimensional body. An experienced tattooist has lots of troubleshooting experience in making a client's idea work. Listen to your tattooist and follow the suggestions she makes—you'll be happier in the end.

PLEASING PIERCINGS

As with tattooing, you have to know what you want. While piercing is not quite as permanent as tattooing, every abandoned hole will leave a mark on your body—a glaring reminder of your bad decision. Piercing also carries a greater risk of infection or allergic reaction; being aware of the safety and aftercare issues involved in piercing has a lot to do with a successful outcome.

First and foremost, body piercing must be done by a trained, professional piercer (please don't let your friends put holes in your body!). The professional piercer uses a new, disposable, hollow piercing needle for each customer; works with only autoclavable surgical steel tools and jewelry; and follows all contamination-prevention procedures. A professional piercer never uses a piercing gun!

The three creative considerations of piercing are: *location, type of piercing,* and *size of jewelry.*

LOCATION

Piercing locations are broken down into four main categories. They are above the neck, oral, above the waist, and below the waist.

Above the neck includes the most common locations, such as the various ear and nose piercings. They also include some unusual placements, like the bridge of the nose and the eyebrows.

Oral piercings are any that have a portion of the jewelry in the mouth. These are distinguished from above-the-neck piercings because they are harder to keep clean, can be trickier to heal, and involve piercing some sensitive areas that may swell a lot. These include the cheek, the lip, the labret (below the lip and above the chin), and the tongue.

Above the waist refers to the nipples and the navel. These piercings involve extra care to heal, mainly because they are often covered with clothing that can rub against the fresh piercing, aggravating it.

Below the waist means the whole gamut of genital piercings—think of any spot on your crotch and there's probably a piercing for it!

Some piercers won't work below the neck or below the waist, since these piercings require greater expertise. But that doesn't mean that piercings above the neck are a breeze—that's why you must choose a knowledgeable, professionally trained piercer to do *anything* on your body. Ask if they have experience in the piercing you're interested in. Most piercers state in their advertising or somewhere in their studio policy exactly what areas they work on.

TYPE OF PIERCING

Piercings are also distinguished by the kind of *organic matter* the piercer will be dealing with. Different kinds of tissue require different styles of jewelry, piercing techniques, and aftercare.

Soft tissue piercings are done through fleshy or membranous matter, like the earlobe or nipple.

Cartilage is tough, elastic, connective tissue, found throughout the body. Ear piercings like the tragus or conch refer to specific spots along the top of the outer ear, which is made up of cartilage.

Surface-to-Surface is a term used to describe piercings where both the entrance and exit holes are made through the surface of the skin; instead of hanging from your body, the piercing appears to be "sitting" on your skin.

Piercing is generally differentiated in terms of degree of technical difficulty. Some procedures are very simple, low-risk affairs that any trained piercer should be able to perform and that heal (with the proper aftercare) quickly and without problems. Other, more extreme piercings require superior ability and medical knowledge. They must be planned in advance and may require you and the piercer to do a few "practice runs." The healing process could be lengthy and somewhat complex, with you and the piercer both keeping a careful eye on the progress.

There are piercings that seem pretty easy but actually involve a great deal of risk. Nose piercings require a lot of commitment on your part; you must carefully follow the aftercare instructions. Because the nose shares a common blood supply with the brain, an infection in this area can be fatal.

SIZE OF JEWELRY

Along with location and type of piercing, you'll need to consider the size of your piercing.

Not every face, nipple, or belly button can handle every size of jewelry or piercing hole. Some of us are not anatomically equipped for certain piercings. A naval piercing requires a deep innie. Small nipples may not be able to handle jewelry of a sufficient size. Your piercer will measure the place you want pierced with a caliper to determine technically what size jewelry you need.

If the gauge is too thick, you may experience keloid scarring or abscessing because the weight of the jewelry is cutting off oxygen to the tissue.

If the gauge is too thin, your body will reject the jewelry and push it out. Visualize the ears of a woman who has worn wire earrings all of her life—they have a fine scar tracing where the piercing originally was to where it has moved.

If the diameter or length is too large, your jewelry will snag easily on clothes, hair, etc., and can rip out.

If the diameter or length is too small, you may develop keloid scarring and your body may actually *absorb* the jewelry!

Then there's the issue of aesthetically sizing and placing the jewelry. A lot of it is your own personal preference, but listen to your piercer's input.

Tribal tats work best when they complement your shape.
Tattoo by Tattoo Mike, Streamline, San Diego, CA.

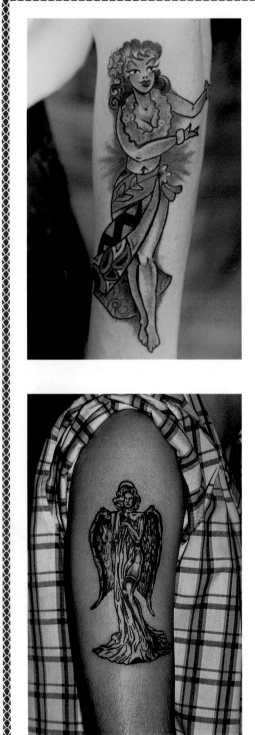

The hula girl is a common Traditional tattoo motif. Tattoo by Albert Sgambati, Lone Wolf Tattoo, Bellmore, NY.

Solid outlining and subtle shading make for good Black and Grey tattoos. Tattoo by Rob Semple, Streamline, San Diego, CA.

Haida designs are a good example of just how interesting flat tats can be. Tattoo by Tattoo Mike, Streamline, San Diego, CA.

Delicate shading gives this Fine Line piece its punch. Tattoo by Dean Semple, Streamline, San Diego, CA.

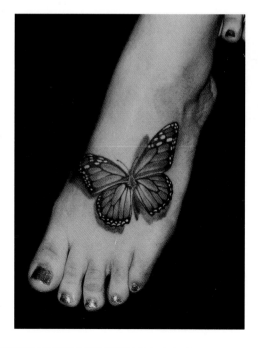

The Mayan figure tattoo (Rob Semple, Streamline Tattoo, San Diego, CA) is a fitting symbol for this serious body mod. Piercings: surface-to-surface (laying on sternum), stretched lobe, eyebrow, and septum.

Amy has a labret, a septum piercing, and many ear piercings, which are examples of an ear project, an eyelet and several lobe piercings. (Photo by Marco Turelli.)

Stacey attaches a chain to her navel piercing (May, Superfly Third Eye, Brooklyn, NY) to spice up the look. Tattoos by Chrystofur, Tattoo Seen, Brone, NY, and Steve, Virginia Beach, VA. (Photo by Mike Martin.)

Tattoo by Rob Semple, Streamline Tattoo, San Diego, CA.

Some fineline artists can achieve astounding detail in very small tattoos. Tattoo by Anil Gupta, Inline, New York, NY.

Artie's full-body tattoo is a real attention-grabber and an example of Oriental tattooing. Tattoo by Andrea Elstoin, East Side Ink, New York, NY. (Photo by Dennis Feliciano.)

A lot of planning goes into a successful cover-up. Tattoo by Nick Wiggins, Mark of Cain, Champaign, IL.

CHAPTER 6
SAFETY
FIRST

WE CAN'T STRESS ENOUGH that *safety and common sense* are the most important considerations in body-art work. Anything that involves penetrating even the outermost layers of your skin must be done with a new needle that is used only once on you and then discarded. A legitimate, well-trained tattooist or piercer follows strict health guidelines and is *happy* to answer any of your questions about her procedures and *show you* her autoclave. An autoclave is the only reliable means of sterilization recognized by the Center for Disease Control. It must be tested monthly by an independent lab to make sure it's working within acceptable levels.

The primary fear most people express about getting tattooed or pierced is that they may contract the HIV virus, which may cause AIDS. HIV is only one of many viruses that can be transmitted. Syphilis, tuberculosis, strep, staph, and hepatitis are just a few of the other diseases to take into consideration. However, professional practitioners of the permanent body arts use Universal Precautions (a set of standards adopted by all medical and related professions). This strict code of practices takes every safety measure so the risk of transmitting HIV or other diseases is virtually nonexistent.

Still, you shouldn't rely on this assurance when you go for body-art work. You must *take responsibility for your own health and welfare.* Ask questions of your tattooist or piercer.

- Have they had any *specific* training in preventing disease transmission?
- Is there an autoclave on the premises and is it tested regularly?
- Do they use disposable, one-use-only needles?
- Is all of their nondisposable equipment made out of sterilizable stainless steel?

If the answer to *any* of the above questions is no, take your business elsewhere.

Look with your own eyes. Here are some important questions that you can answer through your own observations.

- Is the shop clean?
- Is the workstation thoroughly cleaned and disinfected after each tattoo/piercing?
- Are supplies kept in sterile receptacles with lids?
- Is there a covered "sharps" container for disposing used needles?
- Does the tattooist/piercer wash her hands *a lot*?
- Does the tattooist/piercer use latex gloves when working on a client?
- And are those gloves changed if the tattooist has to touch something else during the procedure (including herself)?
- Is the artist clean and sober?

A good body artist appreciates your interest and concerns; it shows that you're committed to getting good, safe work and that you've thought about it beforehand. Many artists will *insist* you watch them set up before the procedure and clean up afterward. They want you to be aware of exactly what they're doing.

If someone makes you feel stupid or uncool for asking a lot of questions about how they do things, they're not the artist for you! You're a paying customer, the way this person makes a living. Anyone who's serious about their work will not be offended, put out, or condescending about your concerns. Remember, it's your body and health that are at stake.

INFECTIONS

There is little risk of your tattoo becoming infected if you choose an artist who meets all of the above requirements, and if you properly care for your new ink (see Chapter 7). Just keep it clean and for heaven's sake don't touch it with dirty fingers! If you notice any swelling, redness, or burning that doesn't go away after a few days, consult a doctor.

Piercings have a greater tendency toward infection because 1) oftentimes the piercing goes through actual flesh, not just between skin layers; 2) bacteria from unsterilized jewelry moves through a fresh pierce like the Germ Express; 3) most people just can't keep their filthy hands off of it! If you just had an operation on your stomach, would you be putting your dirt-encrusted, nicotine-stained paws all over the incision? Then why do you think it's all right to be fingering your new belly ring all day?

Every piercing discharges a little during the initial healing; that's the goo that dries and forms a crust around your jewelry. Once a sufficient layer of tissue forms around the hole, it will stop. Other times, what people perceive as an infection in their piercing is actually a reaction to the cleanser they're using. The area may be inflamed and sore, giving every indication of a low-level infection. Check with your piercer; he may suggest trying a gentler cleansing solution or may tell you not to clean the new hole so often.

What are the signs of an infection? Throbbing pain, a feeling of heat at the piercing site, redness and swelling, or an unusual discharge. These are all pretty normal reactions in a fresh piercing, but they should subside in three to five days. If not, you may have an infection.

Should you develop an infection, *don't remove the jewelry*. Keeping the hole open is the only way for the area to drain. Once you remove the jewelry, your body will close up the hole, sealing the infection inside of you. Don't try to medicate yourself with over-the-counter antibiotics; return immediately to your piercer. If it's not too bad, the piercer will suggest a sea-salt-water soak or maybe an ointment. Your immune system is designed to neutralize pathogenic organisms, so give it a chance. If the infection isn't noticeably better within the twenty-four to forty-eight hours, *go to a doctor*.

Remember, nose piercings are especially dangerous if they get infected. Don't waste any time if you notice problems with that piercing.

ALLERGIES

In tattooing, the greatest potential for an allergic reaction comes from the pigments. Tattoo "ink" is a misnomer, because black is the only actual ink used in tattooing. The rest of the colors are made from mixing dry pigments (made from vegetable matter) with a suspension fluid. Tattoo pigments are seldom reactive to human tissue, although the metallic salts in certain colors can cause a slight irritation in some people. The suspension fluids that are mixed with the pigment may also cause an allergic reaction. Usually the fluid used is water or one of several kinds of alcohol, which are rarely a problem. These risks are slight to none, except to people who have extreme sensitivities already.

Some tattooists use commercially packaged, premixed colors that are made from plastic-based pigments, like acrylic (*It's a floor wax—no! It's a tattoo pigment!*), and complex chemicals. These are much more likely to cause allergic reactions. Still, the potential is pretty slim, and symptoms are generally mild. You can check with your tattooist to see whether she uses plastic or organic-based pigments. If you're concerned about ink allergies, ask your tattooist to do a "patch test" on a discreet part of your body, punching a tiny bit of ink under your skin to see how your body reacts.

Look at it this way: people have been getting tattooed for thousands of years with no ill effects. If you have severe allergies, especially to metals or plastics, consult your physician before getting inked. If you experience any out-of-the-ordinary symptoms (shortness of breath, rapid heartbeat, fever, swelling, a rash, dizziness, etc.) after being tattooed, seek medical attention immediately.

Allergies in piercing come from the type of material the jewelry is made of or the cleaning solution you're using. For your initial piercing, the piercer should use only jewelry made of the highest grade of surgical stainless steel, niobium, or titanium. These metals are preferred because they are the least reactive and won't "leach" any impurities into your body (for more on this see the body-jewelry section in Chapter 4). Some piercers use gold for an initial piercing, but since gold is a highly mixed metal, it's more likely to cause a reaction. If you have a sensitivity to nickel, an element found in both gold and surgical stainless steel, try niobium or titanium.

A FEW MORE WORDS ABOUT
PIERCING SAFETY

There's a much greater risk of damage or infection with piercing than with tattooing—especially when you consider how many untrained people are doing it. Some folks think all they need is a needle or a piercing gun, a piece of jewelry, and *voilà!*—they're a piercer. *Nothing could be further from the truth!* Not only do you run the risk of infection by using unsterilized or improperly sterilized tools, you can also cause permanent damage by "hitting" too deeply or not hitting deeply enough. *Body piercing must be done by a professional!*

Let's start from the beginning. Rule number one: A piercing "gun" is not suitable for any piercing. Not your ears, not your nose, not your navel, not your nipples, not your lip—*nowhere!* Here's why: First, because of the way piercing guns are made, they can *never* be properly sterilized. Even if the part that touches you can be removed and autoclaved, the rest of the gun cannot, so it's a breeding ground for a million living microorganisms that can cause disease. Second, guns pierce by blunt trauma, ripping out a jagged wound of flesh with a dull-ended stud. This immensely increases the chance of infection, rejection, and scarring.

Any piercing you get should be done by a trained professional (and renting a shop in the mall does not qualify one as a professional!). As in tattooing, some people receive their training by apprenticing with a "master piercer." Others attend instructional programs, such as the ones offered by the Gauntlet and Fakir Musafar (see appendix). They may even have varying degrees of medical training. A piercer must have knowledge of anatomy (nerve and capillary paths), dermatology (physiology and pathology of the skin), and biology. Keep in mind, your body's natural reaction is to *reject* any foreign object. Piercing works on the theory of "tricking" your body, through a complex combination of:

- depth and width of the piercing;
- proper gauge and diameter of the jewelry;
- purposely building up scar tissue around the new hole;
- precise timing in the use of an antibacterial (or not).

Without these skills, the artist won't be able to coax your body into accepting the piercing and your system will do everything it can to force it out.

Professional piercers use latex gloves, sterile surgical-stainless-steel piercing tools, and disposable hollow piercing needles. They must know proper techniques so that the pierce isn't crooked, ill-placed, or uncomfortable for the wearer. They must have enough anatomy knowledge to know where you can be pierced and where you can't, and they must know how to manage infection, scar tissue, and events that could occur during the healing process.

Many people who sell jewelry (and not necessarily acceptable piercing jewelry) also offer "full body piercing." Even if they're using disposable, hollow piercing needles instead of a gun, they may have little or no training. These people are very dangerous! *Please* get all of your work done by a *trained piercing professional.*

CHAPTER 7

PROCEDURE AND AFTERCARE

YOU MUST BE EIGHTEEN years old to get a tattoo or piercing. Not just because that's the age of legal consent, but also because most of your physical growth has stopped at that point. Your tattooist/piercer will ask you to sign a legal waiver and he may ask you to produce ID if there's any question as to your age.

It's a good idea to eat a light, healthy meal two to four hours before your appointment. If that's not possible, drink some juice or nondiet soda before your appointment to keep your blood sugar level up. *Never* go to a tattooist or piercer under the influence of alcohol or drugs. Any professional artist will kick your butt to the curb if you show up high.

Wear appropriate clothing. If your piece is going to be covered by an article of clothing, make sure it's loose fitting and made of light, soft material. Be clean. You're going to have to refrain from the bath and shower for a bit after the procedure—and you don't want to offend your artist, right?

The initial steps in prepping for a tattoo or piercing are much like prepping for an operation—and the same precautions for infection control and contamination prevention (called Universal Precautions) are observed. Anything that will come into direct contact with your skin is either:

- disposable—used only on you then discarded, or
- sterile—the few tools that aren't disposable are steril-ized in an autoclave after each use

To begin, the artist puts on latex gloves. The artist must be careful not to spread potential infection by touching *any-thing* that could possibly contaminate you or that could be contaminated. Tattooists and piercers go through several pairs of gloves to do one piece. Something as inconsequential as scratching their noses or answering the phone means a new pair of gloves.

One final word of advice: a conscientious, well-trained tattooist or piercer washes her hands *a lot*!

TATTOO PROCEDURE

Once you've decided on your tattoo, discussed design and placement with the artist, the actual procedure can begin. First the tattooist shaves the area where the tattoo will be placed with a disposable razor. No matter where you want your new ink, there *will* be shaving involved, since tiny hairs cover our entire body. Then, using paper towels, the area is cleaned with an antiseptic solution. Another paper towel is run across a stick of clear deodorant and then applied to your prepped skin. The deodorant is what makes the stenciled image stick to your skin. It also allows the image to be quickly and completely wiped away if the placement isn't right.

Depending on where the tattoo is to be placed, the artist may ask you to stand with your arms and legs straight, to see exactly how the piece will "lie." Because of the way muscles wrap around our body, our skin is constantly twisting. If you lay your arm flat out on a table, your skin will be in a differ-ent position than if your arm hangs down your side. The tat-tooist will place the tattoo with you in a natural stance.

Once the exact positioning has been determined, the tattooist carefully presses a stencil of your design onto your skin and then slowly peels it off. Now you've got a purple outline of your impending tattoo. Look long and hard at this outline to make sure it's exactly where you want it; once the tattooing starts, there's no stopping!

Some tattooists draw freehand, directly onto your skin, without using a stencil. This is okay if you trust your artist one hundred percent, but it's always good to get things down on paper first. This way you and the tattooist both agree, in advance, on exactly what the design will look like, down to every little squiggle and dash. When your stenciled design has dried, you're ready to be tattooed.

The tattooist will put everything that's needed for your tattoo out on a tray. Petroleum jelly, disposable ink caps filled with every color in your tattoo, packets of needles, the tattoo machine. Once everything has been set up, the tattooist must put on disposable latex gloves. Anything that will come into direct contact with your skin is either used once or, in the case of the ink, placed in small, throwaway containers. *All needles must be disposable, and used only once.*

After a little petroleum jelly is traced around the stencil design (to help the tattoo machine glide easily over your skin), the tattooist will find a starting point and, with one hand, stretch that patch of skin out taut. With the other hand, the needle configuration (the number of needles used to achieve a certain effect) is dipped into the tattoo pigment.

The tattoo machine looks like, and is sometimes called, a "gun." An electrical current provides enough power to push the tattoo needles through your skin. The needle configuration (it could be one or more, and several different configurations can be used in one tattoo) is placed in a tube that the tattooist has autoclaved ahead of time and is attached to the end of the tattoo machine. By pressing a foot pedal, the needle(s) move quickly in and out of the end of the tube, mak-

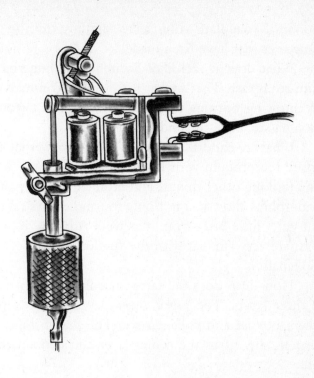

ing approximately three thousand punctures per minute. There's a very distinctive noise to a tattoo machine. The buzz has been compared to everything from a dentist's drill to a swarm of angry bees. That sound is a big part of the tattoo experience, so get used to its high, whining pitch.

Now it's magic time. The tattooist presses the machine to your skin and outlines the design. Initially, it looks like the ink is going everywhere, but don't panic. As the tattooist proceeds, the extra ink will be blotted off and you'll see a nice, clean line. You'll also see little dots of blood emerge from the freshly tattooed spot, but don't worry, there's seldom any more than just those few tiny bubbles. How much you bleed has a lot to do with your personal physiology as well as outside factors (like the presence of alcohol in your bloodstream, which can make you bleed like a stuck pig). Usually your blood will coagulate within a few minutes, clotting up the tiny punctures that have been made.

What does it feel like? Scratch your fingernail on your skin, really fast. That's what it feels like. You may experience an annoying burning sensation during your tattoo, but that soon passes, once the endorphins kick in.

What are endorphins? They're hormones that bind to the opiate receptors in your brain. They reduce the sensation of pain (among other things) and produce a feeling of euphoria. Endorphins allow you not only to handle physical discomfort but get a little buzz from it as well! Athletes, especially runners, are very familiar with the "endorphin rush." So are tattoo fanatics.

How deep does the tattoo needle go? Skin is composed of three layers. The *subcutaneous* layer is the deepest; that's where our fat and collagen are. The *dermis* (also called the *corium* or *cutis*) is the center layer and contains nerve end-

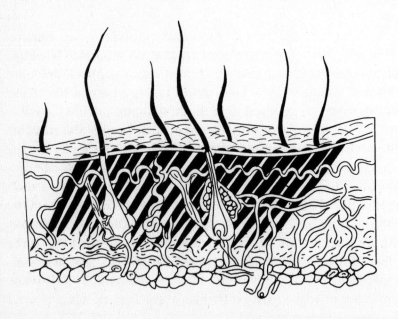

ings, sweat, sebaceous glands, and blood and lymph vessels. The *epidermis* is the outer layer and contains the cells that manufacture pigment and provide immunological defense against foreign substances. The tattoo needle punctures between the epidermis and the dermis.

You'll notice during the tattooing that your skin becomes raised and irritated. This is normal and it, too, will pass. Your tattooist can soothe your skin with cool water during the tattooing process to help alleviate irritation.

Depending on the size and complexity of your piece, the tattoo can take anywhere from thirty minutes to a few hours, even a few sessions! A lot of people try to push their tattooist to finish big pieces in one sitting, but generally it's not a good idea for you or the artist to go longer than a few hours, without at least a break. Just think of what *you* feel like when you sit, intently focused, on something complicated and important for long periods of time. If you want the best work for your money, then stop when the tattooist needs to stop and come back another day. You can't rush perfection!

When your tattoo is finished, the artist will clean it gently with an alcohol/water solution. Once that dries and little blood bubbles have ceased rising to the surface, the artist may want to snap a few photos of your piece. These photos may be used for the tattooist's own records, put on her studio walls or in a portfolio with other work she's proud of, or possibly sent to a tattoo magazine for publication.

If the artist wants to take pictures of your piece, be sure and ask what she plans to do with the photos. Some people don't like to have their tattoos displayed in a studio or in a magazine because they don't want other people copying their designs. Others are very proud of their work and want the whole world to see their skin art! Either way, you have the right to know exactly what your tattooist plans to do with the pictures.

Once the area has been cleaned, the tattooist will apply a light coat of A and D ointment or a comparable emollient. This salve helps repair the damage done to your skin and aids in the healing process. The tattooist may have a tube of A and D ointment to sell you; otherwise, you can find it at most pharmacies. The tattooed area will be loosely bandaged with surgical gauze and medical tape. Some tattooists cover fresh tattoos in plastic wrap—this is *not acceptable*! Even though your new tat needs to be protected, it also needs to breathe. To say nothing of the fact that plastic wrap is a breeding ground for nasty bacteria that could infect your tender new artwork. If you've just gotten a large piece of work, you may want to pick up a few bandages and some medical tape as well, since you might need to change your bandage.

TATTOO AFTERCARE

Aftercare instructions vary slightly from tattooist to tattooist. Your artist *must* give you written instructions for the care of your new piece. Here are the basic things to remember.

1. Depending on the size of the piece and your tattooist's advice, you need to leave the bandage on anywhere from four hours to overnight.
2. When it's time to remove the bandage, do so *very gently*. Slowly peel back the dressing, and if it sticks at all, *stop*! Pour cool water between the skin and bandage. Don't stick your tattoo under a full-force tap. Remember, easy does it. Wait a few minutes and try again. The cold water should loosen your skin from the bandage without yanking the color out.

   During the entire healing process, you must be very careful not to pull any skin or scabs off because you'll also pull the ink out. This will leave uncolored holes in your tattoo.

3. Once you get the bandage off, wash your tattoo very gently *with your fingertips. Do not* use a loofah, sponge, washcloth, cotton ball, paper towel, or anything else but your fingers. *Do not* stick your tattoo under a full-force tap. If you're taking a shower, *do not* let the water directly hit the tattoo. If you're taking a bath, *do not* submerge your tattoo in the water. Use a mild antibacterial soap or any other gentle soap free of deodorants, skin softeners, or other additives. Rub gently, rinse gently.

4. After you've cleaned the tattoo, gently pour cold water over it for a few minutes. The cold water will tighten your pores, which helps the tattoo heal more healthily and quickly, and some tattooists believe it helps the color "set."

5. Lightly pat the tattoo dry with a soft towel.

6. Carefully apply a light coating of A and D ointment. Don't smear it on too thick, because your skin needs to breathe. Smothering your skin with ointment will cause your tattoo to scab up a lot and it could increase your chance of infection. You can use Bacitracin or even a very gentle, additive-free lotion in a pinch (as long as it's *water-based*), but since A and D ointment contains nothing but skin-healing vitamin A and vitamin D, it's the ideal balm.

   Depending on your tattooist's instructions, you may need to apply another bandage. If so, put it on very loosely. You don't want it to stick to your tattoo.

7. For the next two weeks, when you shower or bathe, keep your tattoo away from the water as much as possible. When washing it, use only your fingers. Blot it dry with a soft towel.

No rubbing, scrubbing, picking, or scratching—no matter how much it itches!

For the next two weeks, avoid swimming (ocean or pool), hot tubs, Jacuzzis, and tanning beds.

For the next two weeks, stay out of the sun.

Once the ink has settled into your skin, you can return to life as usual. Always use a strong sunblock on your tattoo when you're going to be outside for any length of time, because the sun's rays will fade your tattoo (there's actually a sunblock on the market designed specifically for tattoos). Also, just like the rest of your body, your tattoo will look better longer if you get into the skin-lotion habit.

If, after the tattoo is fully healed, you're not happy with the way it looks (the color is patchy or has holes, the lines are crooked), *go back to the tattooist*! Artists want to do the best job they can for you and most of them will happily touch up a piece once it's set.

Piercing Procedure

The first step in the piercing procedure is for the piercer to examine the area to be pierced. Measurements are taken in order to select the proper jewelry dimensions. Once this has been determined, you can choose your jewelry based upon the piercer's recommendations.

After the area to be pierced has been thoroughly cleaned, the placement of your piercing (entrance and exit holes) is marked with a nontoxic marker. Some piercers use a toothpick dipped in nontoxic coloring to eliminate any chance of contamination.

The piercer will have everything that's needed set up on a nonporous work surface (a stainless-steel tray, for example), covered with a paper towel or dental bib. You may see some pretty scary tools, but rest assured, the only thing going into your skin is a hollow needle and your jewelry. If your piercer doesn't tell you, ask for an explanation of each tool's use. A caliper is used to take the measurements. Pliers are used to open and close the jewelry (if you're getting a ring). Forceps are sometimes used to clamp onto the area that's going to be pierced. That's not so scary, is it?

The piercing is done with disposable, one-use-only, hollow needles, which have been beveled and sharpened. They are usually about two or three inches long. The needle stays in its sealed package until the piercer is ready for it.

Some piercers use a one-use-only, sterilized cork on the exit side of the pierce. This gives support to the area to be pierced and prevents any unwanted pokes with the needle. Other professionals frown on this practice because it gives piercers a false sense of security—and a false sense of their ability. A technically elegant piercing is done with as few "crutches" as possible.

The exact piercing method depends on the jewelry and the pierce. Generally, a hollow receiving tube is placed on the entrance mark. The needle goes into this. One good push and the needle is through! Your jewelry fits into the hollow end of the needle so that there is no loss of "contact." That means the initial hole the needle makes is followed immediately by the jewelry, since it's attached to the needle. If a piercer loses contact, the piercing has been botched. This needle/jewelry configuration is pushed through your new hole until the jewelry is in place.

Let's talk about pain for a minute. Most people find that the *anticipation* of pain is a thousand times more stressful than the actual piercing sensation. The most common response to a piercing is, "Is that it?" You can do a lot to alleviate not only any actual pain, but the anxiety of anticipating pain, by remembering one simple thing: *breathe*. When nervous or excited, we tend to forget to breathe properly. Take deep breaths: in through the nose, out through the mouth. In through the nose, out through the mouth. This is a very helpful mantra to repeat and practice when you're getting pierced.

Anesthetics of any sort are not recommended for piercing. Anesthetics can cause an allergic reaction, inflammation, and *pain*. Many people feel that piercers who use anesthetic are just trying to hide their own incompetence.

Good piercers will provide an almost pain-free piercing experience. They'll talk you through the entire process, making sure to ask how you're doing as they go. A piercer's soothing voice and friendly manner goes a long way to reducing anxiety. The artist will also pick up on your breathing pattern and perform the piercing as you exhale, which helps alleviate the shock. He'll thread the needle and jewelry through as quickly as he can.

Lots of folks don't consider what happens during a piercing "pain"; they call it a *sensation*.

When it's all over, sit for a minute, or two, or more. The piercer will give you a mirror so that you can see your new body art—fantastic!

PIERCING AFTERCARE

Never touch your piercing unless you're cleaning it. *Always* wash your hands with antibacterial soap before you touch it.

Your fresh piercing may be itchy, swollen, secreting a light-colored fluid, or bleeding a little for the first few days. That's all perfectly normal. The piercing may get crusty, making rotation (turning) of jewelry difficult. Loosen your crust with a hot compress (a damp, clean washcloth, cotton swab, or sterile gauze) and immediately proceed to your aftercare regimen.

As with tattooing, aftercare instructions vary among

piercers—and among piercings. Your piercer *must* give you written instructions for the care of your *specific* pierce.

Here's a rundown of the general steps for aftercare of your new piercing.

1. Clean your piercing twice a day, never more than that. Excessive cleaning can actually hinder the healing process. If you feel you absolutely must clean it more than twice in a day, use a sea-salt (*not table salt*) soak or compress. Add a quarter teaspoon of sea salt to a cup of warm water.

2. Your piercer will recommend an antiseptic appropriate for your specific piercing. After you've removed any crusties, clean the area with the antiseptic and gently rotate the piercing so that the antiseptic gets inside.

3. Wear loose, light clothing over your pierce. Try not to bend, twist, or otherwise move the pierced area any more than necessary. For nipple piercings, keep them covered in a loose T-shirt when you sleep. For genital piercings, women and men may find it a good idea to wear a panty liner. This will absorb any moisture.

4. Keep body fluids away from your fresh piercing, even your own. The one exception is your urine, which is sterile to your body. Use latex barriers to protect genital piercings during sex even if you usually don't.

5. In the case of oral piercings, if you smoke, eat, or put anything in your mouth, rinse with an antibacterial mouthwash, diluted fifty percent with water, afterward.

6. You may find that taking vitamin supplements helps speed up the healing process. Vitamin C and zinc, as well as a good multivitamin, seem to work well.

7. No matter what the primary healing time is, you must wear your initial jewelry (unless your pierce requires

downsizing) six to ten months before you can even think about changing it.

8. Keep following your aftercare instructions even if the pierce looks healed. (Primary healing may only take a few months, but a piercing doesn't completely heal for a couple of years.)

Here are some approximate primary healing times for different piercings:

Ampallang	4–8 months
Apadravya	4–8 months
Cheek	2–4 months
Clit	1–2 months
Clit hood	1–2 months
Dydoes	2–6 months
Ear cartilage	2 months–1 year
Earlobe	6 weeks–2 months
Eyebrow	6 weeks–2 months
Frenum	2–6 months
Guiche	2–6 months
Inner labia	1–2 months
Labret	6 weeks–2 months
Naval	6 months–2 years
Nipple	2–6 months
Nostril	2 months–1 year
Outer labia	2–4 months
Prince Albert	1–2 months
Scrotum	2–6 months
Septum	6 weeks–2 months
Tongue	1 month–6 weeks

CHAPTER 8

HOW TO FIND THE
RIGHT ARTIST

FINDING THE RIGHT PERSON to do your work is very important to a successful piece of body art. Remember, this is the only body you have and you should not cut corners when choosing an artist. If you're not "in" the body-art scene, how do you locate that special artist? The following are ways to make a body-mod connection.

READ THE RAGS, BUY THE BOOKS

There are a number of body-art magazines and books on the market. Unfortunately, you'll only find bits and pieces in each of them, so be prepared to look through a lot of material before you get the information you need. The best ones will educate you, inspire you, and expose you to a wide variety of work from artists all over the world.

Some magazines are story-driven; they profile artists and fans, feature articles on the history of body art, and address technical and safety concerns. Others are more like picture books; they contain photographs of different tattoos, piercings, or pages of designs, and they usually identify the artists. Make sure you look through a magazine before buying it to see if it's got what you need in it.

BE A PEST

Start paying attention to other people's work. Whether you like the piece or not, ask about it. (It's good to know which artists suck as well as which ones shred.) Who did the work? Is the artist local? How long ago did he have the piece done? Would he recommend the artist to other people? Most folks don't mind talking to you about their work, especially if they know you're interested and appreciative and not just an annoying geek (*"Uh, did that hurt?"*). Tattoo/piercing fans are usually very opinionated about artists, styles, and trends—they have a lot to say on these subjects because they themselves enjoy learning and sharing information about body art.

VISIT LOCAL SHOPS

With very few exceptions, tattoo and piercing establishments are set up so that you can stop in and look around. There is a "front" person whose job it is to answer all your questions, and photo albums full of the artists' work for you to examine. Often, flash designs cover the walls and there may be a reference library full of books that the artists use as design sources.

When you walk in, make it clear you just want to check out the studio. Any professional establishment will respect your curiosity and not mind your taking a few minutes to look around. If a studio won't let you look around or answer your questions, they're probably too busy to accommodate you at that moment. In that case, ask when would be a good time for you to come back. If they're just giving you attitude or blowing you off, you probably don't want to give them your business anyway—unless you *like* being treated badly.

There are a few things you should keep in mind when visiting a studio. First of all, don't go snooping around unless you ask! Studios generally have a specific waiting area that's separate from their work area; respect the artists' and customers' privacy. As discussed in Chapter 6, you *do* want to see how clean the environment is, if they have an autoclave, and maybe even watch the artist work—but get permission before you go exploring.

Ask to see examples of the artist's work. There should be photos on the walls or in an album that show tattoos/piercings the studio has done. A lot of studios have more than one artist available, so make sure you know whose work you're looking at when you go through a shop's portfolio. Use the guidelines in Chapters 2 and 5 on Styles of Body Art and Getting Good Work to see if a given artist is the right person for you.

A word of caution: Some studios cut pictures out of magazines and put them on their walls or in their photo albums, but the pieces are not their work, they're just examples. If you ask them if the work is theirs, they may say, "No, but we can do something just like that." Maybe they can, maybe they can't. If you're not familiar with a particular artist's capabilities, it's much better to go by concrete examples of his work instead of undocumented promises.

Body artists are as diverse a group as they come. While plenty of tattooists and piercers are versatile and skilled in many different styles, there are also quite a few that specialize. Some tattooists only do a specific type of skin art, and some piercers won't do certain piercings. Make sure the artist has experience in exactly what you want.

CONVENTIONS, EXPOS, AND SHOWS

A great way to see many of the artists in your area, as well as artists from all over the world, is to attend one of the many annual body-art conventions, expos, and shows. These events take place over a long weekend and are held in a hotel or large meeting hall. Different artists set up portable tattoo booths in an auditorium or ballroom, or work out of their hotel rooms. The conventions follow the strict guidelines set up by the hosting city's local department of health as well as the convention's sponsors, so there's little risk of unsterile conditions.

You can either pay a one-day entrance fee or purchase a pass for the duration of the event. If you're interested in attending a convention in a city other than your own, there are usually special hotel and airfare packages offered for convention goers.

What happens at these events? Lots of tattooing and piercing! But people don't go just to get work done. There are also vendors selling T-shirts, jewelry, books, and other body-art-related merchandise. And there are tattoo contests. For a registration fee, you can enter your tattoo in a competition. There are different categories (for example, Best Realistic, Best Overall Female, Best Small Tattoo) and prizes can be cash, trophies, or both.

Many people who want work by a specific artist seek that artist out when she attends a convention in their area. It's a good idea to set up an appointment ahead of time, though, as a lot of other people may have the same idea.

It's also great fun simply to absorb the atmosphere. You can watch artists in action, see samples of their work (in photos and on live skin), and talk body art until you're blue in the face.

Certain artists charge more for their services at conventions than at their own shops, because they need to recoup their travel expenses. If you're never going to have another opportunity to get the work done, then it may be worth paying the higher price. If the tattooist or piercer is within traveling distance of your home, though, you may want to wait until you can get to his studio.

However, it's ill-advised to start a piece at a convention, with an artist from a different area, that won't be finished that weekend. There are some poor souls walking around out there who have back pieces from two years ago that aren't completed because the artist never came to town again!

Some conventions advertise that "stars" of the body-art world will be *attending* their event, but that doesn't always mean they'll be *working* at the event. Check this out ahead of time if you're trying to get work from a living legend.

You can find information about conventions, expos, and shows in tattoo magazines, in local alternative newspapers, and at area studios.

CONSULTATIONS

If you've found a person whom you feel is capable of giving you the body art you want, you may still wish to have a consultation before committing your flesh to her. In fact, many artists insist on a consultation before they start the work. This allows all the details to be worked out before actually sticking the needle to you. Consultations are mainly used for custom-designed tattoos, but it isn't unheard of in the piercing world.

Usually a deposit is required at the time of your consultation, which is then applied to the final cost of the tattoo. This is a way for the artist to be assured that you're committed to the work and not wasting his or her time.

Bring visual examples of your design idea to the consultation. The more visual input the tattooist has, the easier it will be to render the design exactly the way you want it. The artist may need a little time to work on your tattoo design, so don't be surprised if you have to come back *again* to okay the final design! And don't be afraid to speak up if you're not satisfied; communication is very important to making sure you get what you want.

Just keep in mind that the artist has certain criteria for doing a *good tattoo* that are a lot different from doing a good drawing. You may ask for things that the tattooist knows won't "translate" well onto your skin. You're paying this person to give you a great piece of art—listen to him!

APPOINTMENTS

Some studios take "walk-ins" (where you just show up and have the work done right then) and some require you to make an appointment. If you make an appointment, *keep* the appointment—don't cancel at the last minute. Remember, this is how your artist makes a living. If she reserves three hours of her time for you and you don't show, that's three hours she could be working on someone else, making money!

UNDERGROUND ARTISTS

A few places do not look favorably upon body art (tattooing is illegal in some cities, counties, or even states in the U.S.) and therefore artists are forced to be very discreet or work completely "underground" (no shops with signs out front). This makes finding a competent tattooist or piercer much more difficult. Not only is it harder to locate the artists, but you can't be sure they're following adequate safety precautions because they're not monitored by the local department of health.

Most shops have much stricter safety guidelines than their local health department requires anyway. The majority of underground artists follow these rigid regulations, which are based on *industry* standards that are more thorough and informed than the local authority's. If you follow the tips laid out in this book, you shouldn't have any problems. That doesn't mean there aren't some dangerous scratchers out there, but there are also plenty of good artists forced to work underground due to state or local law. Some artists who work underground don't *want* their profession legalized. They feel by opening the craft up to any jerk with the money to start a shop, then that's just what will happen—any jerk with the money to start a shop, will!

If you live in a place where body art is banned, you can still locate artists using the methods outlined above. Word of mouth is an underground artist's primary means of advertisement. In one sense, this means they'd better be pretty good, otherwise no one will ever bother to track them down! Underground artists often leave flyers or business cards at local businesses connected with the body-art scene—bike and skate shops, clothing and record stores, bars and such. They may even take out small ads in local alternative rags. They also show their work in magazines and attend area conventions.

PROFESSIONAL ORGANIZATIONS

There are national and international organizations for professional body artists. Many of these organizations require their members to have taken classes in preventative measures and safety procedures, as well as to prove they have an on-premises autoclave. Membership to one of these organizations doesn't necessarily mean the artist is great or even that she follows Universal Precautions, but it does give you a place to start. A few of these organizations are listed at the end of this book.

CHAPTER 9

MEHNDI, SCARIFICATION, AND OTHER PRACTICES

As MENTIONED THROUGHOUT THIS book, many types of body art and body modifications are being practiced today. Some are based on ancient rites and traditions and some are as new as the latest medical procedures. Here are a few examples of the options available in the wild and wonderful world of body art.

MEHNDI

Mehndi is an Indian tradition of decorating a woman's hands and feet with henna dye. Originally it was done to celebrate her wedding. These days women from New Delhi to Calcutta have Mehndi designs applied as often as they have their nails done. Traditionally, the patterns are very intricate, and it takes many hours to complete a design. Since Mehndi is pretty much the same texture as the henna dye we use on our hair, it requires a very steady and skilled hand to turn something the consistency of mud into a beautiful, ornate design. The henna dye lasts anywhere from ten days to six weeks, and the color varies from deep brown to reddish brown to orange, depending on your particular chemical makeup.

Mehndi is becoming a very popular form of body art in the West, and shops are opening up in large American cities where you can have any kind of design put anywhere on your body. It's becoming one of the hottest body-art trends of the late nineties, since it's not as temporary as body paint or as permanent as a real tattoo. There's no pain involved and the work can be done anywhere on your body. It's a good idea to select parts of your skin that don't bend or move a lot, as this movement will wear the color off.

BODY PAINT

This temporary body art has evolved quite a bit since Goldie Hawn had *Sock It to Me* scrawled in tempera paint on her stomach in the sixties. A good example of how far body painting has come can be seen on the *Vanity Fair* cover that featured a nude Demi Moore wearing a suit made of body paint. Beautifully executed designs can be just as wild as you want them, since they wash right off!

TEMPORARY TATTOOS

Even temporary tattoos have come a long way since the days of "Lick N' Sticks" that came with boxes of Cracker Jacks. Today there are lots of different designs, some of which are created by real tattoo artists. The best temporary tattoos are made on special paper (like rice paper) with cosmetic ink. They're waterproof and last about one to two weeks, depending on how you care for them. Some people get temporary tattoos in the place where they want a real one so that they can see how it looks. Other people are just tattoo wannabes and slap on a temporary tattoo to temporarily be perceived as cool.

Pretty lame, but hey, it's all about expression, right?

SCARIFICATION

Some body mods are taking their skin art a step further by using scars as decorations. Scarification is done two basic ways: by branding the skin with a hot piece of metal or by cutting it with a scalpel. This is not an exact art form. The results vary, based on the ability of the person who does the work, your body's own ability to raise keloids (fibrous scar tissue), and how much melanin (the natural pigments in your skin) you have. If you have dark, lasting scars from past injuries, then you probably have sufficient melanin to give lasting color to a scarification.

As with any other permanent body modification, this procedure *must* be done by a professional. The professional will know how deep to cut, how long to hold the hot brand to your skin and how to heal your wounds—an interesting subject in itself, because you're not really trying to "heal" these marks, the whole point is to leave a big scar! A professional will also spend *a lot* of time making sure you really want a scar before giving you one.

Branding is done by fashioning pieces of metal into a design, then heating those pieces of metal and applying them to your skin. The burn will spread two to three times the width of the brand, which the design must compensate for. Each strike only lasts a few seconds, and yes, it hurts. Does it hurt when you touch hot metal? Well, then it will hurt when hot iron touches you. People who have been branded speak about the incredible endorphin rush they get (sometimes they go into a low level of shock!)—and the incredible pain they feel once the endorphins wear off. We *are* talking about second- and third-degree burns here. There is a great risk of getting an infection if the brand isn't properly cared for. Third-degree burns actually heal more easily, because the wound is cauterized.

One well-respected body artist has been sculpting intricate "brands" using a surgical laser. The precision of the laser gives the artist more control, making an even line and a cleaner heal.

Cutting is most often done with a surgical scalpel. The sharp blade allows for a more delicate scarring than branding, so you can achieve fine lines and intricate patterns. The person performing the cutting may take a piece of paper and lay it over the design, making a "blood rubbing" of the piece. After the initial cut heals, some people go over the line again (and again) to achieve more depth. Pain is minimal, compared with branding. One New York artist uses a tattoo machine loaded with different needle groupings (but no ink) to achieve a variety of scar shapes and sizes. Much like the laser procedure described above, he gets much more control over the final outcome this way.

Darker skin tends to scar up better, producing heavier keloids (fibrous scars) and more melanin (our natural pigment) in the wound. Since the point is to raise scars, the healing process can involve purposely irritating the wound by introducing a foreign substance or picking at the scabs. Once again: kids, don't try this at home. If you're interested in scarification, find a pro.

AESTHETIC DENTISTRY

Aesthetic dentistry refers to creative techniques that are done to the teeth to change their appearance. Creative dentistry is nothing new. Gold, silver, and porcelain caps are pretty common ways to hide imperfections and generally "jazz up" your mouth. The metal caps can be stamped with your initials or a symbol, and "tooth-toos," little wax designs stuck on your caps, can be added for extra pizzazz. There are more radical procedures such as having a hole drilled into a tooth and then implanting a jewel into the hole for a truly *dazzling* smile. You can have your teeth filed to points—just the canines à la Dracula or all of them, à la the Wolfman. For the less adventurous, porcelain vampire fangs that you can wear temporarily are all the rage.

EXTREME BODY MODIFICATION

Some people change their physical bodies in other ways that are familiar or really push the envelope of body art. These alterations can be as common as muscle training and plastic surgery or as radical as extreme tissue modification and implants.

You can change the physical shape of your body in many ways. Lots of people work out or do muscle training to sculpt their bodies into a desired shape. Plenty of people undergo plastic surgery or have implants to alter their appearance.

While some of the following procedures may seem very radical, keep in mind that many conventional procedures such as removing ribs to make your waist smaller, injecting collagen into your lips to make them fuller, or implanting saline bags in your chest to make it bigger may seem very strange to other people.

Some people bind parts of their body to change their shape either temporarily or permanently. The most common form of this is corset or waist training, which involves wearing a cinch or corset for a certain period of time every day to remold your middle. People who are into this kind of modification keep track of their waist measurements, noting the diminishing size. Reduction can be achieved quickly and temporarily by tightly lacing a corset or cinch—your "wasp" waist will last only as long as you're wearing the gear—or permanently by slowly cinching in your garment while you increase the period of time you wear it. There is a potential danger of damaging your internal organs or bones, so read up on the subject before actually starting the process.

Extreme tissue modification refers to surgical procedures that reshape your body in a radical way. One way of doing this is by implanting foreign material under your skin. This could be metal spikes that stick up out of the top of your skull (which, believe it or not, more than one person has done!) or inserting marbles in your skin between the dermis and the muscle fascia.

One legendary body modifier has created a flap on his stomach about half an inch wide and two inches long—much like a belt loop. Under general anesthetic, two incisions were made. The resulting "flap" was then lifted away from the abdominal wall and the remaining gap was sewn shut by suturing the two incisions together. Since the top and bottom of the flap are still connected to the main body of tissue, blood still circulates through it—if it didn't, the modification would have never healed. Through this flap he sticks a plug, a feather, or any cylindrical object . . . occasionally he hangs his keys from it!

BODY PLAY

Body play takes many forms. It can be temporary piercings or cuttings that are done for a specific event and then removed. It can be more intense, like body suspensions, where piercings are made in key points on your body, chains are attached to the jewelry, and you are then lifted off the ground, suspended by your piercings. Body play has roots in many different religious ceremonies performed by different cultures around the world, and people who partake in these extreme forms of body play usually do so for their own spiritual or sexual reasons.

CHAPTER 10

GETTING RID OF
YOUR WORK

EVEN THOUGH THE PURPOSE of this book is to guide you toward body art that you'll enjoy forever, you may already have an atrocious piece of work that you're dying to get rid of. Are you one of those people who is forced to wear socks with sandals so that no one sees the horrible Tasmanian Devil on your ankle? Does your *new* girlfriend start fuming every time she sees the name of your *old* girlfriend on your chest? That pot leaf inked on your arm doesn't seem like such a good idea now that you're trying to get a job, right? There's nothing worse than having to live with a mistake that you're constantly reminded of every time you look in the mirror. If you've got ink that you just can't bear any longer, the options are either touching up/covering up the tattoo, or removing it.

TOUCH-UPS AND COVER-UPS

Some tattoos just need a little new life breathed into them. If you're basically happy with your piece but think it needs a little work, you can have the tattoo touched up. A common reason for a touch-up is that the lines are bad or blotchy, or the ink was laid in unevenly. A good tattooist can repair these

122

problems without totally losing the original piece. Also, since the tattoo will fade over time, some fresh color will make it look like new again.

You can also perk up a droopy piece by adding on to it. You can add more detail to an existing piece or surround it with new work that ties in to your original design. This is a good way to "camouflage" a crappy tattoo, but keep in mind that the new ink will look fresher and brighter than the old.

If you want to go for a complete cover-up, there are a few things to consider. The more complex the piece is, the harder it will be to cover. A good tattooist maps out the colors and lines of your existing tattoo and then designs a new piece that corresponds to the old one. For example, if your old tattoo had brown at the top and yellow at the bottom, the new one—while being a completely different design—will also have to be a dark on top and a darker color on bottom. The reason is that you can't cover dark pigment with a lighter pigment, although some tattooists will suggest the method below.

Some tattooists may suggest spending a few initial sessions covering your old tattoo with flesh-colored pigment. This gives the tattooist a "cleaner palette" to put the new piece on. However, flesh-colored pigment is not a solution— it's just a preparatory step before getting a cover-up. Flesh colors never blend in enough to look natural, especially if you have light skin. Certain inks—namely black—do not cover well with white or light colors. Still, your tattooist could suggest part, if not all, of your tattoo be prepped in this manner before doing the actual cover-up.

Plenty of bad tattoos get covered up in Tribal designs because Tribal is most often done with black ink; since it's abstract, it can be shaped to cover practically any design. The unfortunate thing is that, like hair in a can, *it usually looks just like what it is.* Hey, sometimes there's just not a whole lot of leeway in masking a bad tat.

LASER REMOVAL

Removal of tattoos is achieved through four basic methods: acid peels, which burn off layers of skin with chemicals; dermabrasion, which involves scraping off the skin layers; surgery, wherein the tattoo is actually cut out of your skin; and laser removal. Since the first three methods leave dramatic changes in your skin color and/or scarring, we'll concentrate on laser removal.

A laser removes tattoos from the skin by rapidly pulsing a specific wavelength of light onto the area. These wavelengths pass through the top layers of skin and are absorbed by the cells that hold the tattoo pigments. Because the light is flashing so quickly, it breaks up these pigment-filled cells, which are then flushed out naturally by your body.

The procedure requires an initial consultation (usually free) by a dermatologist who is also a trained laser surgeon. The doctor will try to determine how successful removal of your tattoo will be and estimate how many sessions it will take. Since tattoo pigments are not regulated by the FDA, there's no standard in pigment consistency, making it pretty hard for the doctor to predict exactly how well the laser-removal treatment will work or how many sessions your piece will require. Most tattoos require anywhere from two to eight treatments, spaced four to six weeks apart, to give the pigment time to be completely flushed out of your body. The precise number of treatments will depend on exactly what kind of tattoo pigment was used, how big the piece is, how deeply it was poked into the skin, and how many different colors are in the tattoo. Obviously, a big, multicolored piece will be more difficult to remove than a small, black one.

Also, certain colors respond better to laser removal than others. The general consensus is that the darker the color (blue, black) the better the chance of total removal. Red and yellow are difficult colors to remove. There are many different types of lasers, each specializing in certain treatments, and new ones are being introduced all the time. Ask your doctor which laser she uses and what colors it's most effective on. As is the case with getting a tattoo, you'll need to do a little research to find the person best suited to remove a tattoo.

The removal process can be a little painful. Most people liken it to being snapped repeatedly with a rubber band or being splattered with tiny drops of hot oil. Local anesthetic is used in some cases, but if you could stand the rapidly pulsing needles that put the pigment into you in the first place, you should be able to handle the rapidly pulsing light used to remove it.

During the session, you (and the doctor) will have to wear safety goggles to protect your eyes from possible damage. The laser component itself is a monstrous machine that has a swing-arm attachment through which the laser is emitted. The doctor holds the end of this swing arm to direct a very fine beam of light onto your skin and controls the laser pulse with a floor pedal. Each procedure lasts only a few minutes. Afterward, an antibacterial ointment and bandage will be applied to the treated area. Keep the area clean and use any ointment the doctor gives you. You can bathe the area the following day, but don't scrub the spot.

You may notice some scabbing and your skin will look a little lighter in the treated area. Your skin's natural pigment will return in a few months. Laser removal works best on light-skinned people; the darker you are, the more likely you'll experience a permanent change in skin color. Laser removal is not recommended for people with very dark skin, although advances in treatment are being made all the time and some doctors are reporting success with dark-skinned patients.

Laser removal is a costly and lengthy procedure that doesn't guarantee total removal of the tattoo. A lot of people who get crappy tattoos removed end up putting new work in the same place to camouflage traces of leftover pigment. Better to be sure about the tattoo you're getting in the first place.

PIERCING RIPS, TEARS, AND SCARRING

If you rip or tear your ear, you can have the spot sewn up. The longer you wait, the more difficult it will be to eliminate successfully, because scar tissue will start building up. Sometimes plastic surgery is required to repair really bad tearing or scarring.

One of the most common cosmetic problems associated with piercing is keloid scarring. Keloids can be removed by a dermatologist or plastic surgeon, but there's no guarantee that more scar tissue won't develop in the same spot! Keloiding is a hereditary condition; if you're predisposed to keloid scars, they may very well return.

Steroid and cortisone injections have been used by some dermatologists to reduce the size of a keloid. This lets you keep the jewelry in place, but the keloids don't disappear entirely.

If you notice the development of a keloid, try using hot compresses and massage with vitamin-E oil. Massaging will help break up the fibrous tissue so that your body can remove it naturally. This doesn't happen overnight. In fact, it's kind of an ongoing battle. As a keloid develops, you may break it down with massage and then—*boom!*—another one pops up! Consult your piercer.

APPENDIX

INTERNATIONAL DIRECTORY
OF BODY ART

THE INTERNATIONAL DIRECTORY OF Body Art includes shops from all over the world. It is in no way complete, but it's a pretty hefty start. *This is not an endorsement* of the shops; it's simply a listing. You'll still have to do your homework.

Body artists tend to move around a lot. We've tried to make this directory as up-to-the-moment as possible, but don't blame us if you find your favorite artist has developed a travelin' jones and moved on.

Studios that pierce, or offer both tattooing and piercing, are delineated by one asterisk (*). Museums, archives, schools and organizations are delineated by two asterisks (**).

Alabama

Jimbo's House of Stain	Biham	AL	205-841-7911
A Tattoo Workshop	Birmingham	AL	205-251-8288
Branding Iron Tattoo	Birmingham	AL	205-836-8287
Rainbow Tattoo	Boaz	AL	205-593-1130
Rainbow Tattoo	Gunterville	AL	205-582-4713
Magic Needles Tattoo	Huntsville	AL	205-830-0102
Wicked Tattoos	Huntsville	AL	205-881-8070
LA Body Art	Mobile	AL	334-479-8889

Buzzard & Sons	North Port	AL	205-339-8461
* White Foot Tattoos & Body Piercing	Ozark	AL	334-774-5288
Riverside Tattoo Studio	Riverside	AL	205-338-1500
Gulf Coast Tattoo	Theodore	AL	334-653-8063

Alaska

AK Tattoo	Anchorage	AK	907-276-1404
Anchorage Tattoo	Anchorage	AK	907-561-0065
Dragon Ray's	Anchorage	AK	907-272-8287
* Lindsey's Tattoo & Body Piercing	North Pole	AK	907-488-8282

Arizona

Silver Eagle Tattoo	Apache Junction	AZ	602-871-9699
Blue Dragon Tattoos	Flagstaff	AZ	520-323-2817
Dr. Julien's Custom Tattooing	Flagstaff	AZ	520-773-4966
Artistic Skin Designs	Mesa	AZ	602-655-1344 or 345-1884
Body Art Tattoo Studio	Mesa	AZ	602-668-7622
Captive Steel	Mesa	AZ	602-668-7622
Dutchman Tattoo Studio	Mesa	AZ	602-641-7204
Lou's Skin Art	Mesa	AZ	602-834-4646
Skin-n-Soul	Mesa	AZ	602-644-0812
Artistic II	Phoenix	AZ	602-233-2442
Artistic Skin Designs	Phoenix	AZ	602-230-8333
AZ's Tattooland	Phoenix	AZ	602-230-1947
Blue Dragon Tattoos	Phoenix	AZ	602-973-4093
Crawling Squid	Phoenix	AZ	602-433-9008
Electric Needle	Phoenix	AZ	602-995-5928
Epidermal Intrusions	Phoenix	AZ	602-278-1037
* HTC Body Adornments	Phoenix	AZ	602-278-1037

HTC Body Jewelry	Phoenix	AZ	800-HTC-JEWL
* HTC Body Piercing	Phoenix	AZ	602-278-1037
Superior Tattoo Equipment	Phoenix	AZ	602-278-4444
Enchanted Dragon	Sierra Vista	AZ	520-459-0500
Club Tattoo	Tempe	AZ	602-902-0943
* HTC Body Adornments	Tempe	AZ	602-784-4460
Living Canvas Tattoos	Tempe	AZ	602-829-6966
Skin Alive	Tombstone	AZ	520-457-9268
Ancient Art	Tucson	AZ	520-747-7545
Big Brother Tattoo	Tucson	AZ	520-388-9091
Enchanted Dragon	Tucson	AZ	520-323-2817 or 326-7807
* G-Nation	Tucson	AZ	520-984-0608
Kick Ass Tattooing	Tucson	AZ	520-574-9760
Old Towne Tattoo	Tucson	AZ	520-323-6966
Skin Art Salon	Tucson	AZ	520-325-7140
Skully Bros Tattoos	Yuma	AZ	520-329-8588

Arkansas

In the Skin Tattoos	Conway	AR	501-329-0344
Tattoos by Wild Child	Fayetteville	AR	501-582-9055
Tattoos by Charlie	Ft. Smith	AR	501-648-1579
Santa Cruz Tattooing	N. Little Rock	AR	501-753-0960
Back Roads Tattoo	Russellville	AR	501-890-6396
Express Yourself Tattooz	Searcy	AR	501-279-0345
Tattoos by Wild Child	Siloam Springs	AR	501-524-4257
Two Guns Tattoos	Siloam Springs	AR	501-524-4858
JD's Body Art	Trumann	AR	501-483-6875

California

Alburn Tattoo	Alburn	CA	916-890-1556
Claremont Tattoo Studio	Alta Loma	CA	909-624-4253

GTC's Tattooland	Anaheim	CA	714-827-2071
Kari Barba's Outer Limits	Anaheim	CA	714-761-8288
Primitive Basic	Anaheim	CA	714-761-8488
Wheeler's Itchy Ink Boutique	Anaheim	CA	714-520-4610
Indigo Skin Design	Antioch	CA	510-778-9069
Lost Coast Body Art	Arcara	CA	707-825-7537
Fine Line Tattoo & The Tribal Weaver	Auburn	CA	916-889-1556
All American Tattoo Co.	Bakersfield	CA	805-325-0350
California Tattoo	Bakersfield	CA	805-322-5692
Skinworks	Balboa	CA	714-675-8905
International Tattoo Garden	Belmont	CA	415-594-0590
* Twodays Jewelry	Benicia	CA	707-747-0941
Blue Buddah	Berkeley	CA	510-549-9860
** Paul Rogers Tattoo Archive & Research Ctr.	Berkeley	CA	510-548-5895
Zebra Tattoo	Berkeley	CA	510-649-8002
Primal Instinct	Burbank	CA	818-842-2071
Chez Nazee	Carmichael	CA	916-972-1111
Empire Tattoo	Cathedral City	CA	800-254-8288
New Creations	Chico	CA	916-898-8287
* Sacred Art Tattoo & Piercing	Chico	CA	916-343-9337
Tattoos by J & D	Colati	CA	707-795-2611
Cheri's Unique Tattoos	Concord	CA	510-685-4221
Superior Tattoo Studio	Costa Mesa	CA	714-646-0333
Bad Body Body Grafix	Coyote	CA	408-463-0200
Ray Gun	Dana Point	CA	714-496-7021
Ink Spot Tattoo Parlor	El Sobrante	CA	510-222-8332
* John Lopez Body Piercing	Eureka	CA	707-444-3497
* Primal Decor	Eureka	CA	707-445-2609
SkinSignea	Eureka	CA	707-443-3809
Tattoos by Tenacious Eye	Felton	CA	408-335-7222

World Class Tattooing	Fresno	CA	209-224-2270
Tattoo Tavern	Ft. Bragg	CA	707-961-0257
** Triangle Tattoo & Museum	Ft. Bragg	CA	707-964-8814
Classic Tattoo	Fullerton	CA	714-870-0805
Flying Tiger Tattoo Club	Fullerton	CA	714-996-2095
Romo Ink	Fullerton	CA	714-870-1505
Electric Ink Inc.	Garden Grove	CA	310-327-7765
Flesh Merchants Tattoo	Garden Grove	CA	714-636-5763
Tattoo Magic	Garden Grove	CA	714-530-0444
Body Shop Tattoo	Glendale	CA	818-956-TATU
* Back Door Body Piercing	Grass Valley	CA	916-274-0663
Joker's Wild	Harbor City	CA	310-534-4532
* Gauntlet	Hollywood	CA	313-657-6677
* HB Tattoo & Piercing	Huntington Beach	CA	714-374-4880
Flesh Skin Grafix	Imperial Beach	CA	619-424-8983
** Dermalogical Institute & Research	Irvine	CA	714-775-3767
* Wicked World	Isla Vista	CA	805-683-1803
The Ink Cup	Joshua Tree	CA	619-366-2870
Darrell's X-Calibur Tattoos	La Habra	CA	800-683-9924
Tattoo Gallery	La Habra	CA	818-333-9924
Laguna Beach Tattoo	Laguna Beach	CA	714-497-3702
Sick & Twisted	Laguna Beach	CA	714-376-0036
Gypsee's Studio of Art	Lancaster	CA	805-949-0622
Psycho City Tattoo	Lancaster	CA	805-949-7649
Lou's Tattoos	Lemoore	CA	209-925-1553
Charlotte's Web	Livermore	CA	510-449-6165
* HTC's Somatic Body Piercing	Long Beach	CA	310-438-6406
Body Electric	Los Angeles	CA	213-954-0408
Dave Zero Tattoo	Los Angeles	CA	213-464-6031
Easyriders Tattoo Studio	Los Angeles	CA	213-658-8817
Funny Farm	Los Angeles	CA	213-913-7043

* Gauntlet Piercing	Los Angeles	CA	310-657-6677
Lite & Bold Tattoo	Los Angeles	CA	818-763-7828
Melrose Tattoo	Los Angeles	CA	213-655-4345
Oceanic Tatau	Los Angeles	CA	213-626-7817
Purple Panther Designs	Los Angeles	CA	213-882-8165
Rose & Dagger Tattoo	Los Angeles	CA	213-722-3522
Skin Graffiti Tattoo	Los Angeles	CA	213-358-0349
Spotlight Tattoo	Los Angeles	CA	213-871-1084
Sunset Strip Tattoo	Los Angeles	CA	213-650-6530
Tabu Tattoo	Los Angeles	CA	310-391-5181
Tattoo Mania	Los Angeles	CA	310-657-8282
West Coast Tattoo	Los Angeles	CA	213-629-8101
* XII B.C.	Los Angeles	CA	213-782-9069
* Tattoo Time	Mariposa	CA	209-742-6013
* Mystical Body	Modesto	CA	209-527-1163
Modern Tattoo	Moreno Valley	CA	909-924-2232
Flying Colors Tattoo	Napa	CA	707-226-8986
Newport Tattoo	Newport Beach	CA	714-673-5118
Skin Works	Newport Beach	CA	714-675-8905
Studio M	North Highlands	CA	916-339-0331
* Sierra Tattoo & Piercing Co.	Oakhurst	CA	209-683-INKS
Sacred Skin Tattoo	Oakland	CA	510-636-1168
Ace Tattooing	Ocean Beach	CA	619-222-5097
* Fountain's Tattooing & Body Piercing	Oildale	CA	805-399-4688
Studio 1482	Pacific Beach	CA	619-270-1482
Flesh Dreamz Tattoo	Pacoima	CA	818-890-5582
Everybody Body Accents	Palm Desert	CA	619-340-1331
In the Skin	Pasadena	CA	818-683-8789
Incognito Tattoo	Pasadena	CA	818-584-9448
Old Towne Tattoo	Pasadena	CA	818-577-1732
Shannon O'Sullivan	Pasadena	CA	818-441-3256
Hangtown Tattoo	Placerville	CA	916-642-9172

*	Bodyworks Skin Art & Piercing	Pomona	CA	909-629-3221
	Jimi's Tattoo Parlor	Port Hueneme	CA	805-488-9190
	Darkside & Tattooing	Redding	CA	916-246-1773
	Empire Tattoo	Rialto	CA	909-875-2833
	Above All Tattooing	Sacramento	CA	916-349-9235
	Backdoor Studio	Sacramento	CA	916-927-2136
	California Tattoo Co.	Sacramento	CA	916-723-3559
	Liberty Tattoo	Sacramento	CA	916-344-4340
*	Studio M Tattoo & Piercing	Sacramento	CA	916-338-0979
*	Sub-Q	Sacramento	CA	916-446-9777
*	Exotic Body	Sacto	CA	916-447-OUCH
	Avalon Tattoo	San Diego	CA	619-274-7635
	Big City Tattoos	San Diego	CA	619-299-4868
	Blue Dragon Tattoo	San Diego	CA	916-544-0075
	Eric's Human Engraving	San Diego	CA	619-689-2690
	Hillcrest Gallery	San Diego	CA	619-299-7452
	Inker's Tattoo Co.	San Diego	CA	619-286-8282
	Lucky's Tattoo Parlor	San Diego	CA	619-338-9460
	Master Tattoo Studio	San Diego	CA	619-239-2684
	Pacific Tattoo	San Diego	CA	619-544-1121
*	Primal Art Body Piercing & Jewelry	San Diego	CA	619-222-6986
	San Diego Tattooland	San Diego	CA	619-223-8930
	Streamline Tattoo	San Diego	CA	619-272-8286
*	Superfly West Tattoo & Piercing Studios	San Diego	CA	619-234-3597
	Tattoo Gallery	San Diego	CA	619-299-7452
	Tattoo Ink Spot	San Diego	CA	619-483-0028
**	Association of Professional Piercers	San Francisco	CA	415-281-9648
*	Body Manipulations Piercing	San Francisco	CA	415-621-0408
	Diamond Club	San Francisco	CA	415-776-0539

Erno's Tattoos	San Francisco	CA	415-431-4645
Everlasting Tattoo	San Francisco	CA	415-928-6244
* Gargoyle	San Francisco	CA	415-552-7393
* Gauntlet Piercing	San Francisco	CA	800-RINGS2U or 415-431-3133
Goldenfield's Tattoo Studio	San Francisco	CA	415-433-0558
** Lyle Tuttle's Tattoo Museum	San Francisco	CA	415-775-4991
* Nomad Body Piercing Studio	San Francisco	CA	415-563-7771
Picture Machine	San Francisco	CA	415-668-7377
Soul Scars	San Francisco	CA	415-931-1016
Tattoo Blue II	San Francisco	CA	415-826-6969
Tattoo City	San Francisco	CA	415-433-9437
Van Go Tattoos	San Francisco	CA	415-621-6096
Body Adornments	San Jose	CA	805-544-8765
Marks of Art Tattoo	San Jose	CA	408-377-1924
NewSkool Studios	San Jose	CA	408-279-0927
* So. Cal. Tattoo & Body Piercing	San Pedro	CA	310-519-8282
Area 51 Tattoo	San Rafael	CA	415-455-8367
** Golden State Tattoo Assoc.	Santa Ana	CA	714-894-2168
* Obscurities	Santa Barbara	CA	805-682-6838
Tattoo Santa Barbara	Santa Barbara	CA	805-962-7552
Dawei Tattoo	Santa Clara	CA	408-983-0833
* Staircase Tattoo & Body Piercing	Santa Cruz	CA	408-425-7644
* Good Art Company	Santa Monica	CA	310-452-7602
* SM 316	Santa Monica	CA	800-613-0316
Bert's Santa Rosa Tattoo	Santa Rosa	CA	707-526-0471
Secret Raygun Tattoo	Santa Rosa	CA	707-575-0610
Body & Soul	Sherman Oaks	CA	818-784-7528
Tattoo Til the Cows Come Home	Sonora	CA	209-533-0890

Dakota Steel	Soquel	CA	800-995-0595
* Cliff Cadaver Body Piercing	Studio City	CA	818-980-5994
Studio City Tattoo	Studio City	CA	818-769-4049
Neverland Tattoo	Sunland	CA	818-352-9785
Yoni Tattoo	Tarzana	CA	818-996-9152
Soul Expressions Tattoo	Temecula	CA	909-694-5379
Truckee Tattoo	Truckee	CA	916-587-4559
** American Inst. of Permanent Color	Tustin	CA	800-772-4728
Realistic Tattoo	Twenty Palms	CA	619-367-0552
Tattoo Heaven	Ukiah	CA	707-462-6502
Classic Tattoo	Upland	CA	909-949-7971
Empire Tattoo	Upland	CA	800-254-8288
* Puncture Body Piercing	Upland	CA	909-981-2877
Six Feet Under Tattoo	Upland	CA	909-949-0157
Bill's Tattoos	Vallejo	CA	707-649-1841
Red Genie Tattoos	Vallejo	CA	707-649-1545
** Society of Permanent Cosmetics	Vallejo	CA	707-557-1012
Ink, Ink.	Venice	CA	310-314-7703
Tattoo Image	Victorville	CA	619-951-7322
Flying Dog Tattoos	Visalia	CA	209-738-0864
Electric Pencil Tattoo	Whittier	CA	310-946-4888
Gina's Studs & Tattoos	Yuba City	CA	916-674-5732
Twin Cities Premier Tattoo Art	Yuba City	CA	916-671-1738

Colorado

American Tattoo Studio	Aurora	CO	303-341-4974
Tattoo Shop	Aurora	CO	303-755-2800
Boulder Tattoo	Boulder	CO	303-444-7380
Bound by Design	Boulder	CO	303-786-7272
* K & K Jewelry	Boulder	CO	303-444-5602

Calamity Jane's Tomboy Tattoos	Carbondale	CO	303-963-0745
Art with a Pulse	Colorado Springs	CO	719-635-8801
Enchanted Dragon II	Colorado Springs	CO	719-540-0320
Pikes Peak Tattoo	Colorado Springs	CO	719-632-6141
American Tat 2	Denver	CO	303-322-4048
Body Creations	Denver	CO	303-355-9018
Bound by Design	Denver	CO	303-830-7272
Emporium of Design	Denver	CO	303-333-4870
Tattoo by Mickie	Denver	CO	303-430-7927
Rocky Mountain Tattoo	Englewood	CO	303-761-4468
Millennium Gallery of Living Art	Ft. Collins	CO	970-482-8282
* Blazing Trails Tattoo & Body Piercing	Grand Junction	CO	970-241-1266
Skibo's Tattoo	Greeley	CO	970-356-6772
American Tattoo	Lakewood	CO	303-238-3602
Lady of the Lake Tattoos	Loveland	CO	970-635-1909
Body Graphics	Northglen	CO	303-254-4473
Slowhand Tattoo Works	Sheridan	CO	303-794-8288
Ace Tattoo	Thornton	CO	303-427-3527

Connecticut

Full Moon Tattoo	Danbury	CT	203-791-9205
Peter Tat 2	Danbury	CT	203-790-7045
Skin Deep Tattooing	Danielson	CT	203-779-1174
Guide Line Tattoos	E. Hartford	CT	203-289-2698
* Papillon Studio	Enfield	CT	203-745-2050
Flat's Tattooing Inc.	Groton	CT	203-448-6844
The Dark Side Tattoo	New Haven	CT	203-469-9208
* Studio Zee Tattooing	New Haven	CT	203-787-2773
Derma-Flicks	Norwalk	CT	203-847-6859
Screemin' Mimi's Electric Art	Pomfret Center	CT	203-928-4454

TNT Body Graphics Tattoo Emporium	S. Windsor	CT	203-289-6534
Full Sail Tattoo	Stafford Springs	CT	860-684-0488
Living Art Studio	Stafford Springs	CT	203-684-6266
Tony's Tattooing	Stamford	CT	203-969-7079
Body Art Inc.	Torrington	CT	203-496-1292
Tattoo Int'l	Wallingford	CT	203-949-1678
Rainbow Body Art	Waterbury	CT	203-596-9396
Wizards Advanced Tattooing	Willington	CT	203-429-4014

Delaware

Little Gary's Tattooing	Dover	DE	302-678-0409
August Moon Tattoos	Glasgow	DE	302-737-5509
Fat Larry's Tattoo Shop	Laurel	DE	302-875-4579
Art Alternative	Wilmington	DE	302-655-2622
New Flesh Tattoo Studio	Wilmington	DE	302-791-9711
Redman Tattoos	Wilmington	DE	302-762-5204

District of Columbia

* Perforations Piercing Studio	Washington	DC	202-289-8863
* The Leather Rack	Washington	DC	202-797-7401

Florida

First Coast Tattooing	Atlantic Beach	FL	904-249-8710
New Oracle	Bradenton	FL	941-362-9675
Tattoo Factory	Brandon	FL	813-661-4893
Artistic Body Works	Cocoa Beach	FL	407-799-1630
Cocoa Beach Tattoo	Cocoa Beach	FL	407-783-8287
Sportsman Tattoo	Crestview	FL	904-689-4577
* Body Designs Piercing	Daytona Beach	FL	904-248-0895

Mr. Happy Tattooing	Deerfield Beach	FL	305-427-3195
Treasure Coast Tattoos	Delray Beach	FL	407-731-0310
Ink Doctor	Fernandina Beach	FL	904-277-6642
Bruce Bart Tattooing	Ft. Lauderdale	FL	954-564-1865
Primitive Harmony	Ft. Lauderdale	FL	954-964-5654
Tattoos by Doc	Ft. Lauderdale	FL	954-938-9887
Tatts Taylor Tattooing	Ft. Lauderdale	FL	954-525-7910
Ancient Art Tattoo Studio	Ft. Meyers	FL	914-995-8282
South Florida Tattoo Company	Ft. Pierce	FL	407-465-0012
Tattoos Forever	Ft. Walton Beach	FL	904-244-5117
Atlantic Tattoo Studio	Harbor Oaks	FL	904-760-4184
Tattoos by Lou	Hialeah	FL	305-828-8944
Electric Body Art	Hollywood	FL	954-989-9065
Inksmith & Rogers	Jacksonville	FL	904-221-8282
* Peacock's Tattoo Studio	Jacksonville	FL	904-745-0011
Tattoos by Lou	Kendall	FL	305-670-6694
Paradise Tattoo	Key West	FL	305-292-9110
Voodoo Tattoo	Key West	FL	305-292-2282
RJ's Tattoo	Lake Worth	FL	407-641-5745
Tattoo Paradise	Lake Worth	FL	407-966-8814
Raven's Rose Tattoo	Largo	FL	813-536-5763
Taboo Tattoos	Leesburg	FL	904-360-1113
Tattoo Time	Maitland	FL	407-331-5928
South Florida Tattoo Co.	Melbourne	FL	407-951-8993
Personal Expressions	Merritt Island	FL	407-454-7399
* Public House/Adam's House	Miami	FL	305-444-3015
Art Attack	Miami Beach	FL	305-531-4556
South Beach Tattoo Co.	Miami Beach	FL	305-538-0104
Tattoos by Lou	Miami Beach	FL	305-532-7300
Merlin's Tattoo	North Miami	FL	305-944-6306
Tattoos by Lou	North Miami	FL	305-944-0888
Ancient Art Tattoo	Orlando	FL	407-855-TATU

Deana's Skin Art	Orlando	FL	407-281-1228
Fred & Peaches Tattoos	Orlando	FL	407-275-5050
The General	Orlando	FL	407-855-8288
Willie's Tropical Tattoo Studio	Ormond Beach	FL	904-672-1888
Ragman's Sharp Art	Pace	FL	904-994-3894
Tattoos by Marty	Palm Bay	FL	407-984-1315
Tattoos Forever	Panama City	FL	904-234-8282
Dragon Master's Ink	Pensacola	FL	904-457-1444
Tattoos Forever	Pensacola	FL	904-455-5678
Bruce Bart Tattooing	Pompano Beach	FL	954-783-2339
Foxes Tattoo Studio	Pompano Beach	FL	954-783-0050
Funhouse Tattoos	Pompano Beach	FL	954-972-4944
Adventurous Art Tattoos	Port Charlotte	FL	941-625-5566
Natural Art Lasting Impressions	Port Richey	FL	813-842-5878
Artistic Designs	Port St. Lucie	FL	407-465-8401
Papillon South Tattoo Studio	Riviera Beach	FL	407-845-9079
Inksmith's Fountain of Youth	St. Augustine	FL	904-825-0108
* Lakeside Therapeutic Massage	Tallahassee	FL	904-552-3098
Artistic Armor	Tampa	FL	813-837-0554
Mortal Images Tattoo	Tampa	FL	813-882-4008

Georgia

Debi Kienel	Acworth	GA	770-975-1718 or 770-445-8000
Midnight Iguana	Athens	GA	706-549-0191
* Pain & Wonder Tattoo & Piercing	Athens	GA	706-208-9588
Ancient Art	Atlanta	GA	404-523-3660
Body Images	Atlanta	GA	404-355-4303
Body Languages	Atlanta	GA	404-355-4303

	Sacred Heart Tat-2	Atlanta	GA	404-222-8385
	Timeless Tattoos	Atlanta	GA	404-315-6900
	Skin Images	Augusta	GA	706-667-0060
	Blackjack Tattooing	Columbus	GA	706-687-5354
	Superior Skin Art	Columbus	GA	706-685-1444
*	Tan Lines & Nails	Douglasville	GA	404-920-0303
	Ink Wizard	Forest Park	GA	404-361-2111
	Ink Wizard	Griffin	GA	770-227-4994
	Ink Wizard	Macon	GA	912-784-1882
	Peacock Tattoos	Macon	GA	912-788-3825
	House of Color	Marietta	GA	770-612-0616
	Optical Illusion Tattoo	Marietta	GA	770-579-0008
	Psycho Tattoo	Marietta	GA	770-977-8287
	Crypt Kicker Boutique & Tattoo	Rome	GA	706-295-4081
	Kingsbay Tattoo Shop	St. Marys	GA	912-882-8007
	Ink Wizard	Stockbridge	GA	770-507-9622
	Black Cat	Stone Mountain	GA	404-292-8192
	Innerself Expressions	Warner Robins	GA	912-329-9639
	Electric Crayon	Warner Robins	GA	912-328-0113

Hawaii

	Rainbow Falls Tatu	Hilo	HI	808-961-2621
	Skin Deep Tattoo	Hilo	HI	808-935-5554
	Aloha Tat-2	Honolulu	HI	808-955-0323
*	Exotic Beauty	Honolulu	HI	808-926-2942
*	Skin Deep Tattooing & Body Piercing	Honolulu	HI	808-924-7460
	Alley Cat Tattoo	Kahului Maui	HI	808-871-7464
	Aloha Tattoo	Kailua	HI	808-263-2019
	Black Cat Tattoo	Kailua	HI	808-263-5535
	Big Island Tattoo	Kailua-Kona	HI	808-329-7384
	Pirates of the Sea	Kailua-Kona	HI	808-329-4450
	Class Act Tattoo	Kihei	HI	808-875-1110

Skin Deep Tattoo	Kihei	HI	808-875-8217
Skin Deep Tattoo	Lahaina	HI	808-661-8531
Happy Dolphin Tattoo	Maui	HI	808-875-1110

Idaho

Garden City Tattoo	Boise	ID	208-344-0804
High Desert Tattoo	Boise	ID	208-338-9927
** Idaho Tattoo Assoc.	Boise	ID	208-344-0804
Ink Vision	Boise	ID	208-383-0912
A Touch of Class	Boise	ID	208-345-9299
Craig's Tattoo	Caldwell	ID	208-455-1012
Living Art Tattoo	Chubbuck	ID	208-237-8288
Artistic Skin Illustrations	Idaho Falls	ID	208-522-5640
Tats & Tails	Lewiston	ID	208-743-8330
Falling Moon Tattoo	Moscow	ID	208-882-4257
* Ty's Tattoos & Exotic Piercing	Pocatello	ID	208-234-4577
War Paint Tattoo	Twin Falls	ID	208-724-9349

Illinois

Skin of a Different Color	Aurora	IL	708-851-9936
Roy Boy's III	Calumet City	IL	708-862-8288
Dragon Master Tattoo	Carbondale	IL	618-529-1929
Golgotha Tattoos	Carbondale	IL	618-529-4809
Lady Hawke Tattoos	Carbondale	IL	618-529-4809
Mark of Cain	Champaign	IL	217-355-9472
Bob Oslon's Custom Tattooing	Chicago	IL	312-248-0242
* Body Basics Tattooing & Piercing	Chicago	IL	312-404-5838
Chicago Tattooing Co.	Chicago	IL	312-528-6969
* Classic Tattoos & Body Piercing	Chicago	IL	312-261-9420

Dream Maker Tattooing	Chicago	IL	312-486-3125
Fat Joe's Jade Dragon	Chicago	IL	312-736-6960
Guilty & Innocent Productions	Chicago	IL	312-404-6955
* No Hope No Fear Tattoo & Piercing	Chicago	IL	312-772-1960
Tattoo Factory	Chicago	IL	312-989-4077
* Tatu Tattoo & Body Piercing	Chicago	IL	312-772-8288
Wizard of Ink	Chicago	IL	312-622-4241
* The Zone Tattooing & Body Piercing	Chicago	IL	312-586-0000
Prairie Tattoo	Chicago Hts.	IL	708-709-0139
Dream Illustrations	Chillicothe	IL	309-274-2877
Doc's Tattoos	Collinsville	IL	618-346-4790
Mike's Tattoos	Danville	IL	217-443-1242
Sign of the Rainbow	Decatur	IL	217-425-4939
Tattoo-U	Decatur	IL	217-428-8710
Skin Graphics	Dolton	IL	312-660-7546
Bodys by Skeet	Dundee	IL	708-551-1986
Elgin Tattoo	Elgin	IL	708-622-0504
* Pores of Color Tattoo & Body Piercing	Frankfort	IL	815-464-7255
Hawk's Tattoo	Galesburg	IL	309-342-0293
RJ's Tattoo	Harvard	IL	815-943-5117
Wolf's Fine Line Tattoos	Joliet	IL	815-723-5918
Flesh & Blood Tattoos	Kewanee	IL	309-854-9203
Pat's Tattoo Studio	Lockport	IL	815-834-0396
Tattoo City	Lockport	IL	815-836-TAT2
Goldie's Tattoo	Loves Park	IL	815-636-0260
Altered Images	Lynwood	IL	708-758-8282
* Tattoo Blue & Piercing I	Macomb	IL	309-833-1849
RD's Tattooing	Marion	IL	618-997-5259
Living Color Tattoo & Novelty	Mattoon	IL	217-234-9611

Living Color Tattoos	Moline	IL	309-797-6966
Flash Factory	Oak Lawn	IL	708-424-7523
Tattoo Teddy's Custom Tattooing	Oak Lawn	IL	708-499-1524
Breezy's Tattoo Studio	Rantoul	IL	217-893-3018
House of Pain	Rockford	IL	815-968-4527
JG's Tattoo	Rockford	IL	815-961-8288
Skin Drawing Tattooing	Rockford	IL	815-963-7972
Tattoos by Panama	Rushville	IL	beeper 800-802-0976
Sarge's House of Ink	Silvis	IL	309-755-7995
Doc Finn's Ancient Art	S. Elgin	IL	708-742-8288
Black Moon Tattoos	Springfield	IL	217-753-4427
* Vision World Tattoo Studio & Body Piercing	Urbana	IL	217-328-7131

Indiana

* The M Plan	Bloomington	IN	812-323-8020
Famous Leg Greg	Gary	IN	219-980-2912
Roy Boy's Place	Gary	IN	219-884-4965
* Body Accents	Indianapolis	IN	317-259-1950
Don's Tattoo Studio	Indianapolis	IN	317-356-5624
Presto Tattoo	Lake Station	IN	219-962-3600
Johnny's World	Michigan City	IN	219-874-1053

Iowa

* Lasting Impressions Tattoo Studio	Ames	IA	515-296-4642
Reflection Tattoo	Des Moines	IA	515-262-9417
Tattoos by Randy	Marshalltown	IA	515-752-0477
Slingin' Ink Tattoo	Montezuma	IA	319-623-3564
Big River Tattoos	Muscatine	IA	319-263-3275
Chuck's A-1 Tattoo	Ottumwa	IA	515-682-3861

Midwest Wade's Custom Tattoo	Sioux City	IA	712-258-1847

Kansas

Skin Art Creations	Baxter Springs	KS	316-856-5938
Fantasy Graphics	Hays	KS	913-625-2626
East Coast Al's	Kansas City	KS	913-321-1214
Skin Illustrations	Lawrence	KS	913-841-8287
Mid America Tattoo	Manhattan	KS	913-539-4482
Ink Slinger Tattoo	Overland Park	KS	913-631-4889
Aces High Tattoo	Wichita	KS	316-733-8595
The Underground	Wichita	KS	316-945-8041

Kentucky

Ink Cave	Bowling Green	KY	502-782-9551
Impressive Tattoo	Danville	KY	606-238-0058
* The Hole Thing	Lexington	KY	606-258-9069
Tattoo Charlie's	Lexington	KY	606-254-2174
Tattoo Charlie's	Louisville	KY	502-964-8774 or 502-366-9635
Ace in the Hole	Owensboro	KY	502-926-9635
Queen of Hearts Tattoo	Radcliff	KY	502-351-4800
Tattoos by the Renegade	Radcliff	KY	502-351-6767
BoDean's Tattoos	Richmond	KY	606-624-0255

Louisiana

Baton Rouge Tattoo Co.	Baton Rouge	LA	504-273-0690
Fantasies in Flesh	Baton Rouge	LA	504-383-3266
Tiger's Claw Tattoos	Baton Rouge	LA	504-924-0690
Psycho Studios	Bossier City	LA	318-741-1005
Art-n-Soul	Kenner	LA	504-464-1617
Electric Expressions	Kenner	LA	504-464-0053

Allen's Ancient Art	Lafayette	LA	318-234-3776
Westbank Tattoo Studio	Marrero	LA	504-341-6781
Doc Don's Studio	Metairie	LA	504-833-0190
Art Accent Tattooing	New Orleans	LA	504-581-9812 or 504-949-5377
Electric Expressions	New Orleans	LA	504-488-1500
Electric Ladyland Tattoo	New Orleans	LA	504-866-3859
* Rings of Desire Piercing	New Orleans	LA	504-524-6147
Blue Moon Tattoo	Pineville	LA	318-640-6666
S & H Tattoo	Ruston	LA	318-254-0350
Fine Line Tattoos	Shreveport	LA	318-425-3990
Bayou Tattoos	Slidell	LA	504-643-3339

Maine

Bar Harbor Tattoos	Bar Harbor	ME	207-288-9722
Wiz Tattoos	Brewer	ME	207-732-3027
Body Graphics	Brunswick	ME	207-729-4051
Fine Line Tattoo	Canaan	ME	207-474-7640
Caveman's Classic Art	Lewiston	ME	207-784-0809
Mad Hatter's Tattoo Studio	Old Orchard Beach	ME	207-934-4090
Milwaukee Iron Tattoo	Portland	ME	207-871-1040
Portland Tattoo	Portland	ME	207-772-4662
Wicked Tattoos	Skowhegan	ME	207-474-9985

Maryland

* Harm City	Baltimore	MD	800-4-MY RING
Tattoo Charlie's Place	Baltimore	MD	410-244-1160
Great Southern Tattoo Co.	College Park	MD	301-474-8820
** Int'l Tattoo Artists Guild	Cumberland	MD	301-729-8282
Hysterical Tattoo	Ellicott City	MD	410-418-9428
Gypsy John's Fine Line	Essex	MD	410-686-7922 or 410-633-2319

*	Torture Chamber	Fork	MD	410-407-7299
**	Alliance of Professional Tattooists	Glen Burnie	MD	410-768-1963
	Dragon Moon	Glen Burnie	MD	410-768-6471
	Gemini Tattoo	Odenton	MD	410-551-9808
	Inkers Dream Wizard Tattoo	Rockville	MD	301-977-0094
	Explosive Tattoo	Salisbury	MD	410-548-9887
	Capitol Tattoo	Silver Spring	MD	301-585-3483
	Fatty's Custom Tattooz	Silver Spring	MD	301-587-4456
	Little Vinnie's Tattoos	Westminster	MD	410-876-4638
	Southern Maryland Tattoos	White Plains	MD	301-645-0306

Massachusetts

*	Rites of Passage	Boston	MA	617-783-1918
*	Di'Orio's Salon	Worcester	MA	508-756-7791

Michigan

	Creative Tattoo As Art	Ann Arbor	MI	313-662-2520
*	Insane Creations	Ann Arbor	MI	313-332-0058
*	Miami Moon Jewelry	Ann Arbor	MI	313-769-7478
	Gash's Graphics	Battle Creek	MI	616-962-4066
	Hamlett's Grateful Tattoo Co.	Benton Harbor	MI	616-927-1432
	Eternal Tattoos	Berkeley	MI	313-425-0428
	American Graffiti	Brighton	MI	810-220-2066
*	Nails by Sharon	Clinton Township	MI	810-468-8830
*	Showtime Clothing	Detroit	MI	313-485-3349
	Jay Wheeler	Detroit	MI	313-780-1682
	The Reverend Dark	E. Lansing	MI	517-332-8305
	Splash of Color	E. Lansing	MI	517-333-0990

Underground Art	Edwardsburg	MI	616-663-7985
Main St. Tattoo	Elkton	MI	410-676-TAT2
* Wolfe's Den Tattooing & Body Piercing	Frederic	MI	517-348-8106
Victor Locke Tattoo Studio	Garden City	MI	313-427-6030
Magnum Tattooing Inc.	Grand Rapids	MI	616-245-1880
Image Art Tattoo Works	Holland	MI	616-355-7016
River House Tattoo	Interlochen	MI	616-275-6457
Chuck's Tattoo	Jackson	MI	517-784-8287
Steele Dreamer Tattoos	Kalamazoo	MI	616-345-1631
Sully's Kustom Tattooz	Kalamazoo	MI	616-345-7979
Forever Perfect Tattoos	Lansing	MI	517-887-6966
Splash of Color	Lansing	MI	517-394-2120
Tattoos by Magic Mike	Lansing	MI	517-332-1202
Almighty Tattoo Revival	Lapeer	MI	313-667-3695
Tribal Image Tattooing	Lapeer	MI	810-667-3292
* Intricate Decor & Body Piercing	Mt. Pleasant	MI	517-773-2713
World of Color	Mt. Pleasant	MI	517-723-5259
Superior Lines Tattoo	Newberry	MI	906-293-5092
Eternal Tattoos	Roseville	MI	810-779-4770
Royal Oak Tattoo	Royal Oak	MI	810-398-0360
Ancestral Marks Tattoo	Saginaw	MI	517-793-1266
Wonderland Tattoo	St. Clair Shores	MI	810-774-8288
Deeper Meanings Custom Tattoo Art	S. Haven	MI	616-637-1611
Ink Asylum	Taylor	MI	313-291-4040
Eternal Tattoos	Waterford	MI	313-673-7110
Ink for Life	Ypsilanti	MI	313-485-8288
* Pirate's Den Tattoo Company	Ypsilanti	MI	313-485-3349

Minnesota

Main Line Tattoos	Anoka	MN	612-427-4008
* Adventures by Lori	Becker	MN	612-261-5743
Bear Nasty Tattoos	Becker	MN	612-261-5275
Marcie's Sharp Images	Blaine	MN	612-786-1699
Shadow Masters Tattooing	Cloquet	MN	218-879-3422
Tattoos by Lee	Coon Rapids	MN	612-427-9771
Body Lines Tattoo Studio	Duluth	MN	218-624-4333
Riverside Tattooing	Elk River	MN	612-441-3894
D & D Tattooing	Faribault	MN	507-334-2029
Ace Tattoo	Golden Valley	MN	612-595-0926
Electric Dragonland Tattoo Studio	Hopkins	MN	612-933-2097
Tattooing by Yurkew	Minneapolis	MN	612-825-6161
Tattoos by Neil	Minneapolis	MN	612-827-8188
Tatu's by Kore	Minneapolis	MN	612-824-2295
Alien's Images & Skin	Owatonna	MN	507-451-8229
Rochester Tattoo	Rochester	MN	507-280-8011
Rising Phoenix Tattoo Studio	St. Cloud	MN	612-255-7305
ACME Tattoo Co.	St. Paul	MN	612-771-0471
Hy-Tone Tattoo	St. Paul	MN	612-224-8217
Tattoos from Grease	St. Paul	MN	612-776-2913
Seaside Tattoo	Spicer	MN	612-796-0022
Lisa LeCuyer	Stillwater	MN	612-351-1094
Tatts by Zapp	Stillwater	MN	612-439-4974
* Tiger Lily Tattoo & Piercing	Stockton	MN	507-689-2953
Cherry Creek Tattoo	Willmar	MN	612-231-0501

Mississippi

Jack & Diane's Kustom Tattoo	Biloxi	MS	601-436-9726

Buzzard & Sons	Columbus	MS	601-327-2901
Gypsy's Exotic Skin Art	Greenville	MS	601-332-3328
Jack & Diane's Kustom Tattoo	Gulfport	MS	601-864-4764
A-1 Tattoo	Jackson	MS	601-372-2800
* Junior's Tattoo & Body Piercing	Meridian	MS	601-483-4049

Missouri

Aloha Nonie Lani's Studios	Branson	MO	417-336-8535
Different Drummer Tattoo	Cape Girardeau	MO	314-651-8688
Alternative Art Studio	Columbia	MO	314-874-8145
Dreamcatcher	Columbia	MO	314-499-1313
Tattoo You	Columbia	MO	314-875-7850
* Extremus Body Piercing	Kansas City	MO	816-756-1142
Grimm's Tattoo Studio	Kansas City	MO	816-531-7622
Shanghai Lil's Tat-2	Knob Noster	MO	816-563-4990
A Touch of Class	Maryland Heights	MO	314-298-9960
* Cheap TRX	St. Louis	MO	314-664-4011
* Goldenlands Tattoos & Piercing	St. Louis	MO	314-423-0530
Eyewitness Tattoo	Springfield	MO	800-TAT ON US
Miller Cotton's Tattoos	Springfield	MO	417-889-8287
Iron Age Studios	University City	MO	314-725-1499
Ultimate Art Form	Wentzville	MO	314-639-5415

Montana

* Eagle Tattoo & Body Piercing	Billings	MT	406-245-0379
Tattoo Art	Billings	MT	406-245-0851
Bozeman Dermagraphics	Bozeman	MT	406-585-0034

Craig's Place	Helena	MT	406-449-3265

Nebraska

Rebels to Roses	Chadron	NE	308-432-3513
Kool Tattoo	Kearney	NE	308-236-5034
Ralph's Hungry Eye	Lincoln	NE	402-477-9279
* Body Mods	Omaha	NE	402-551-8801
Grinn & Barrett Tattoo	Omaha	NE	402-553-7714
Skin Art Tattoos	S. Sioux City	NE	402-494-2919

Nevada

Artist at Large	Fallon	NV	702-423-6285
Cheri's Unique Tattoos	Fallon	NV	702-423-6666
Artforms Tattoo	Las Vegas	NV	702-452-9828
Desert Heat	Las Vegas	NV	702-383-6600
Body Graphics	Reno	NV	702-322-8623
Lasting Impressions	Reno	NV	702-333-6676
Shadow Brite	Reno	NV	702-348-8383

New Hampshire

LA East Studio	Laconia	NH	603-524-6908
Sign of the Wolf	Laconia	NH	603-366-2557
Crows Creations	N. Conway	NH	603-356-5551
White Mountain Tattoo Studio	N. Conway	NH	603-356-0113
Tattoo Fever	Pelham	NH	603-635-3129
Dastardly Dan's	Rindge	NH	603-899-6989
Brothers Too Tattoo	Salem	NH	603-890-8779
Juli Moon Design	Seabrook	NH	603-474-2250
Tattoo America	Seabrook	NH	603-474-9304

New Jersey

Body Art World I	Asbury Park	NJ	908-988-9875
Backstage Tattoos	Atco	NJ	609-753-5799
Fear No Tattoo	Atlantic City	NJ	609-344-0333
Lola's Tattoos	Bogota	NJ	201-488-3234
Tribal Passage	Brick	NJ	908-458-8569
Another Tattoo Shop	Brook Bound	NJ	908-563-1010
Wicked Gypsy Tattoo	Cardiff	NJ	201-383-1833
Tattoo Shoppe	Carlstadt	NJ	201-933-0037
Skin Illustrations	Cookstown	NJ	609-758-1770
Pore-Q-Pin Designs	Dumont	NJ	201-384-2655
Ink Spot I	Elizabeth	NJ	908-352-5777
* Pleasurable Piercings	Hawthorne	NJ	201-238-0305
Spirits & Alchemy	Jersey City	NJ	201-653-5164
Jersey Phil's Tattoo Madness	Kenvil	NJ	201-927-2838
Butch's Skin Art	Keyport	NJ	908-495-4899
Eternal Images	Lanoka Harbor	NJ	609-971-TAT2
Ink Spot II	Linden	NJ	908-862-1722
Ink Spot West	Linden	NJ	908-862-1722
Physical Graffiti	Linden	NJ	908-925-5288
Cherokee Chuck's Tattoo	Lindenwold	NJ	609-782-8866
High Voltage	Lindenwold	NJ	609-627-3468
Lucky Seven	Little Ferry	NJ	201-487-7233
Tattoos by Will	Livingston	NJ	201-992-1997
Body Art World II	Long Branch	NJ	908-222-9740
Body Marks Tattoo	Middletown	NJ	908-291-4562
Ink-Credible Tattoo Inc.	Montclair	NJ	201-783-9633
Powerhouse Tattoo	Montclair	NJ	201-744-8788
Last Rites Tattoo	Montville	NJ	201-402-2380
Shotsie's Tattoo West	Newfoundland/ W. Milford	NJ	201-697-0032
Big Easy Tattoo	Newton	NJ	201-383-6464
Body Art World III	Pt. Pleasant	NJ	908-892-9776

Slingin' Ink Tattoo	Pt. Pleasant Beach	NJ	908-295-2582
Rebel Image	Rio Grande	NJ	609-889-2422
Gina's Tattoo Connection	Toms River	NJ	908-929-9805
Tradewinds Tattoos	Toms River	NJ	908-929-4400
Lion's Den	Trenton	NJ	609-695-8282
Nightmare Productions	Tuckerton	NJ	609-294-2617
* Lee's Tattooing & Body Piercing	Vineland	NJ	609-691-4778
Stingray's Tattoo Odyssey	Washington	NJ	908-689-TATU
Paul's Tattoos	Washton Township	NJ	609-728-4226
Shotsie's Tattoo	Wayne	NJ	201-633-1411
Tattoo Factory II	Wayne	NJ	201-633-7778

New Mexico

Fine Line Studio	Albuquerque	NM	505-255-3784
Jerm-N-Dave's Tattoo	Albuquerque	NM	505-843-7546
Route 66 Fine Line Tattoos	Albuquerque	NM	505-255-3784
VJ's Tattoo Art	Albuquerque	NM	505-884-9770

New York

Bruce Bart Tattooing	Albany	NY	518-432-1905
Dream Weaver	Auburn	NY	315-258-8288
Tattoo Tony's Tattoo Parlor	Auburn	NY	315-252-4123
Avon Tattooing Studio	Avon	NY	716-226-3860
Central New York Tattoo Co.	Baldwinsville	NY	315-638-8288
Artistic Creations	Ballston Spa	NY	518-885-0636
** Body Designs School of Professional Piercing	Bay Shore	NY	516-968-0141

Lone Wolf Tattoo	Bellmore	NY	516-221-9085
Peter Tat-2	Bethpage	NY	516-938-6367
Artful Ink Tattoo	Bohemia	NY	516-589-7399
* Bare Apple Tattoo/ Sugar Mountain Piercing	Brockport	NY	716-637-7790
* Wild Child Piercing Studio	Bronx	NY	718-822-5655
Tattoo Seen	Bronx	NY	718-892-9370
Coney Island Vinny	Brooklyn	NY	718-368-0438
Fly Rite Studios	Brooklyn	NY	718-599-9443
Huggy Bear Tattoos	Brooklyn	NY	718-965-3512
* Modern American Piercing Services	Brooklyn	NY	718-680-9775
Studio Enigma	Brooklyn	NY	718-266-6612
Sunset Ink	Brooklyn	NY	718-714-9422
Superfly Studios	Brooklyn	NY	718-783-8565
* That's the Point	Brooklyn	NY	718-934-4228
Third Eye Productions	Brooklyn	NY	212-726-1550
Tuff City Tattoo	Brooklyn	NY	718-563-4157
* Cowpoke	Buffalo	NY	716-885-0252
Tattoos by Paul Massaro	Buffalo	NY	716-876-6200
Tracy's Tattoo	Buffalo	NY	716-885-5564
MacKenzie's Forever Ink	Carmel	NY	914-225-4147
Tattoos by Tim	Carthage	NY	315-493-6112
* Cliff's Tattoo Inc.	Centereach	NY	516-732-1957
A Touch of Color	Cortland	NY	607-758-3601
Underground Leather & Tattoos	Cortland	NY	607-756-4205
Peter Tat-2	Deer Park	NY	516-254-4390
Richie Tattoo	Elmont	NY	516-488-8282
Physical Graffiti Tattoo Studio	Fairport	NY	716-381-2480
Drew's Tattoo	Gloversville	NY	518-661-5896
* Body Designs Tattooing & Piercing	Hicksville	NY	516-932-5797
Peter Tat-2	Hillsdale	NY	518-325-4667

Wild Side Art	Holley	NY	716-638-1090
Artistry in Ink	Honeoye	NY	716-229-5034
Scratch Tattoo	Jackson Heights	NY	718-803-3103
Painless Steel	Livingston Manor	NY	914-439-3015
Tattoo Fantasy	Marlboro	NY	914-236-3451
* Middletown Tattoo	Middletown	NY	914-343-2972
Big Joe & Sons	Mt. Vernon	NY	914-668-9894
Prospective Dragon Studios	Nesconset	NY	516-724-1925
* Living Art Tattoo	New City	NY	914-638-0362
Abstract Tribal Tattoo	New York	NY	212-388-9060
Alphabet City Tattoo	New York	NY	212-388-9772
* Andromeda	New York	NY	212-505-9408
Anil Gupta Inkline Tattoo	New York	NY	212-614-0094
* Cicada Body Adornments	New York	NY	212-353-0726
Custom Tattoo Art by Elishka	New York	NY	212-260-7279
Denise de la Cerda at Inkline	New York	NY	212-614-0094
East Side Ink	New York	NY	212-388-0693
Fun City Tattoos	New York	NY	212-674-0754 or 212-353-8282
* Gauntlet	New York	NY	212-229-0180
Kaleidoscope	New York	NY	212-274-8006
* NY Beyond	New York	NY	212-274-8006
** New York Body Archive	New York	NY	212-807-6441
Porcupine	New York	NY	212-330-9295
Rising Dragon Graphics	New York	NY	212-645-TATU
Spider Webb Galleries	New York	NY	212-255-1490
Tattoo Spot	New York	NY	212-677-7944
* Venus Modern Body Arts	New York	NY	212-473-1954
Bousson's Tattooing	Norwich	NY	607-336-8611
Peter Tat-2	Oceanside	NY	516-678-6427
The Underground	Olean	NY	716-373-TAT2
Under the Gun Tattooing	Oxford	NY	607-843-9833

* Cliff's Tattoo & Body Piercing	Patchogue	NY	516-447-2253
Precision Tattooing	Pleasantville	NY	914-741-1270
Fat Cat Designs	Queens	NY	718-267-1326
Shades of Autumn	Queens	NY	718-626-5186
Tattoos by Elf	Queens	NY	718-849-5562
Angelina's Cosmic Rainbow Art	Rochester	NY	716-262-6219
Physical Graffiti	Rochester	NY	716-262-4444
Points of Interest	Rochester	NY	716-244-0217
White Tiger Tattoo	Rochester	NY	716-621-4460
* Cliff's Tattoo & Body Piercing	Rocky Point	NY	516-821-1959
* NYC Underground Tattooing	Ronkonkoma	NY	516-696-TAT2
Smoking Gun	Ronkonkoma	NY	516-737-8149
Lotus Tattoo Inc.	Sayville	NY	516-244-TATU
Artistic Tattoos	Selden	NY	516-732-9585
Physical Graffiti	Suffern	NY	914-368-3537
Bruce Bart Tattooing	Tannersville	NY	518-589-5069
Eagle Tattooing	Wappingers Falls	NY	914-298-2070
Peter Tat-2	W. Hempstead	NY	516-292-8622
** Women's Assoc. of Int'l Tattooists	Woodstock	NY	914-679-4429
Pat's Tats	Woodstock	NY	914-679-4429
Shanghai Tattoo	Wurtsboro	NY	914-888-0160

North Carolina

Immortal Images	Charlotte	NC	704-523-1129
* The Shaper's Quest Tattoo & Piercing	Charlotte	NC	704-375-8288
Tattoo Johnny's	Charlotte	NC	704-358-3863
Skin Scene Tattoos	Dunn	NC	919-892-6113
Bill Claydon's Tattoo World	Fayetteville	NC	910-867-9792 or 910-860-0373

Smokin' Guns Tattooing	Fayetteville	NC	910-864-8282
Living Arts Tattoo Parlor	Gastonia	NC	704-867-8679
Skin Art by Randy	Gastonia	NC	704-868-9198
Damn Yankees Custom Tattoos	Goldsboro	NC	919-751-8477
Carolina Tattoo Co.	Greensboro	NC	910-271-2030
Garry's Skin Gra-Fix	Greenville	NC	919-756-0600
Point Blank Tattoo	Hendersonville	NC	704-697-8787
Body Language Tattoo Studio	Jacksonville	NC	910-353-4377
* Sleeping Dragon Tattoo & Piercing	Jacksonville	NC	910-347-9545
Tattoo Doug's East Coast Studio	Jacksonville	NC	910-353-4377
Tattoos by Buzz Jr.	Jacksonville	NC	910-938-3585
Lifestyles Expressions	Kannapolis	NC	704-932-1872
Necro Design Tattoo	Lake Lure	NC	704-625-4187
Skinsations by Sting	Monroe	NC	704-283-1313
Worlock's Southern Dragon	Raleigh	NC	919-233-1760
RC's Tattooing	Statesville	NC	704-871-8985
California Emporium of Tattoos	W. Asheview	NC	704-254-1747
Joker's Wild	Wilkesboro	NC	910-838-4466
Liquid Skin	Wilmington	NC	910-392-3008
Marks of Distinction	Wilmington	NC	910-392-1123
Afterlife Tattoo	Winston-Salem	NC	910-725-6081
Tattoo Joe's Place	Winston-Salem	NC	910-788-6090

North Dakota

Derma Design Tattooing	Bismarck	ND	701-224-1349
* Sterling Rose Tattoos & Piercing	Fargo	ND	701-232-1744
Derma Design	Minot	ND	701-839-4674

Ohio

Aardvark Tattoo	Akron	OH	330-434-8855
* Steady Eddie's Tattoos-n-Piercing	Akron	OH	330-773-1701
Shadowworks Art & Design	Amelia	OH	513-753-8288
Mr. Bill's Tattooz	Ashtabula	OH	216-964-3103
Art Apocalypse	Athens	OH	614-594-8287
Crow Tattoos	Athens	OH	614-592-6193
C & L Tattoo Studio	Bristolville	OH	330-889-2811
Cincinnati Tattoo Studio	Cincinnati	OH	513-921-3308
Designs by Dana	Cincinnati	OH	513-681-8871
House of Tattoo	Cincinnati	OH	513-241-3421
Permanent Productions	Cincinnati	OH	513-281-5800
Uptown Tattoo	Cincinnati	OH	513-281-6968
* Body Work Productions	Cleveland	OH	216-421-7181
8-Ball Tattoo	Columbus	OH	614-784-8850
Jan's Tattoo Shop	Columbus	OH	614-224-6001
Kelly's Tattoo Studio	Columbus	OH	614-231-6528
* Piercology	Columbus	OH	614-297-4743
* Stained Skin Tattoo & Piercing	Columbus	OH	614-297-SKIN
Tattoos by Kevin	Columbus	OH	614-238-0888
Tim & Conni's Fineline	Columbus	OH	614-476-4700
Sacred Art Tattoo	Corvallis	OH	503-752-7463
Big Ed's Tattooing	Elyria	OH	216-324-4360
Living Color Tattoo	Fremont	OH	419-332-8889
Stormer Tattoo	Geneva	OH	216-466-4099
The Body Canvas	Heath	OH	614-522-8201
Squirrelly's Skin Art	Hubbard	OH	216-534-4160
* Get Hooked	Maple Heights	OH	216-581-3906
Customeyes Ink	Mentor	OH	216-974-7966
Taylor Tattooing	Miamisburg	OH	513-847-8842
The Tat Shop	New Paris	OH	513-437-6300
Clean & Sober Tattooing	Sandusky	OH	419-621-0990

Pain & Pleasure Tattoo	Sandusky	OH	419-627-0069
Tattoos R Us	Springfield	OH	513-322-9422
Infinite Art Tattoo	Toledo	OH	419-292-1990
Lady Luck Tattooing	Toledo	OH	419-382-3036
* Living Arts Tattoo & Body Piercing	Toledo	OH	419-382-8805
Toledo Tattoo	Toledo	OH	419-726-1300
Personal Touch	Van Wert	OH	419-238-4157
Fine Lines Tattoo	Wickliffe	OH	216-943-4008
Fingers	Willoughby	OH	216-942-3567
Z Tattoo Studio	Wintersville	OH	614-266-2581
Moving Pictures Studio	Wooster	OH	330-264-8282
Bootleg Tattoo	Zanesville	OH	614-452-2662

Oregon

Tattoo by Design	Eugene	OR	541-485-5520
Tattoo Studio West	Eugene	OR	503-345-8282
Art on U Tattoos	Klamath Falls	OR	503-884-0201
Custom Body Art	Klamath Falls	OR	503-882-0201
Capricorn Dragon	Lebanon	OR	541-529-2202
Culture Shock	Medford	OR	541-772-8282
A 21st Century Studio	Portland	OR	503-255-3784
Atomic Tattoo	Portland	OR	503-224-3633
Attitudes	Portland	OR	503-224-0050
Deluxe Tattoo	Portland	OR	503-774-8477
* Dermagraphics Tattoos & Piercing	Portland	OR	503-224-8416
Infinity Tattoo	Portland	OR	503-231-4777
Sea Tramp Tattoo	Portland	OR	503-231-9784

Pennsylvania

** National Tattoo Assoc.	Allentown	PA	215-433-7261
Fresh Ink Tattoo Studio	Altoona	PA	814-942-9260

Harry's Tattooing	Boyertown	PA	610-367-2202
Hero Tattooing	Butler	PA	412-283-4531
Backstage Pass	Carlisle	PA	717-258-0893
Animal's Tattoo	Carnegie	PA	412-279-2123
Elite Tattooing	Chambersburg	PA	717-263-1409
Skin Flix	Coplay	PA	610-261-1570
M & M Tattooing	Downington	PA	610-269-0760
* Pleasure & Pain Tattoo & Piercing	Easton	PA	610-252-7316
Bay City Tattoo	Erie	PA	814-456-7260
Buddha's Body Art	Erie	PA	814-833-0439
* Jester's Court Tattoos & Piercing	Etna	PA	412-784-8282
Mystic Marc's	Exton	PA	610-363-5166
* Mainline Tattooing	Frazer	PA	610-889-3345
Electric Line Tattoo	Freeport	PA	412-295-9311
Little Nicky's	Hatbro	PA	215-441-8277
Tattoo Universe	Kulztown	PA	610-683-8485
Touch of Ink	Lebanon	PA	717-273-9021
Permanent Impressions	Lemoyne	PA	717-273-9021
Carle Hesse's II	Mansfield	PA	717-662-0734
Mystical Tattoo Emporium	Mayfield	PA	718-876-6322
Island Ave. Tattoo	McKees Rocks	PA	412-331-9226
Hub's Custom Tattoos	Middleburg	PA	717-837-5072
Bob's Tattoos	Montgomery	PA	717-323-4259
Lion's Den	New Hope	PA	215-862-9602
Cool Tats for Cool Cats	N. Huntingdon	PA	412-864-7585
Studio One Dermagraphics	Norwood	PA	610-586-4640
Carle Hesse's I	Perkasie	PA	215-453-0734
Body Graphics	Philadelphia	PA	215-923-5834
Mel's Magic	Philadelphia	PA	215-729-6633
Philadelphia Eddie's Tattoo Museum	Philadelphia	PA	215-426-9977
Pop's Place	Philadelphia	PA	215-338-6270
Tattoo Time	Philadelphia	PA	215-612-9392

Art FX	Pittsburgh	PA	412-364-5522
* Bodyworks Tattoo & Piercing	Pittsburgh	PA	412-731-3462
Cruel & Unusual Tattoos	Pittsburgh	PA	412-574-2745
Inka Dinka Doo Tattoo	Pittsburgh	PA	412-683-4320
Carle Hesse's World Famous Tattooz III	Plumsteadville	PA	215-453-0734
Wizard's World of Tattoos	Pottstown	PA	610-327-0478
Reading Tattoo	Reading	PA	610-376-1444
TNT	Redding	PA	610-944-9009
Sylvester's Skinetic Art	Roslyn	PA	215-885-6106
Marc's Tattooing	Scranton	PA	717-344-4744
Totem Tattoo	Shamokin Dam	PA	717-743-7830
Ink Well	Southampton	PA	215-953-9453
Totem Tattoo	State College	PA	814-237-1355
American Tattoo Co.	Verona	PA	412-828-8661
Gunslingers	Washington	PA	412-745-7735
C.C. Rider's Rocking Tattoos	Waynesboro	PA	717-765-4857
Show Time Tattooing	Whitehall	PA	610-264-7737
Flaming Star	Wilkes-Barre	PA	717-829-8588
Feel the Magic	York	PA	717-846-6818

Rhode Island

Color Creations	E. Providence	RI	401-438-9297
Electric Ink Tattoo Salon	E. Providence	RI	401-435-3393
Galleria di Tatuaggi	Newport	RI	401-847-4155
Art Free Tattoo	Providence	RI	401-454-5640
Artistic Tattooing	Providence	RI	401-861-7373
Inflicting Ink	Providence	RI	401-683-5680
Sin on Skin	Tiverton	RI	401-624-8287
Don's Tattoo Studio	W. Warwick	RI	401-826-2410
Rennaisance Tattoo	Woonsocket	RI	401-769-3384

South Dakota

Black Hills Tattoo	Rapid City	SD	605-399-2929
Black Hills Tattoo	Sioux Falls	SD	605-335-0832
Snake's Tattoos	Sioux Falls	SD	605-336-7466
Tattooing by Gypsy	Sioux Falls	SD	605-334-6683
River City Tattoos	Yankton	SD	605-665-1576

Tennessee

TJ's Tattoo	Chattanooga	TN	615-867-2053
New Needle Tattoo	Columbia	TN	615-381-5244
Smoky Mountain Tattoo Co.	Gatlinburg	TN	615-436-8776
Tattoo Arama	Henderson	TN	901-989-9222
Bear's Den	Jackson	TN	901-423-3689
Mountain Tattoo	Knoxville	TN	423-970-3307
Electric Sting	Maryville	TN	615-681-6681
Downtown Tattoos	Memphis	TN	901-527-5134
Dragon Master's	Memphis	TN	901-383-8875
Mouse's Custom Tattooing	Memphis	TN	901-353-6250
Rocky's Tattooing	Memphis	TN	901-323-8288
* Underground Art	Memphis	TN	901-272-1864
Forever Yours Tattoos	Millington	TN	901-358-4511
Ship to Shore Tattooing	Millington	TN	901-872-0405
Ronnie's Tattoos	Mountain City	TN	615-727-9747
Tattoos by Shane	Mt. Juliet	TN	615-773-8288
No Mercy Tattooing	Murfreesboro	TN	615-893-5444
Fantasy Tattoo	Nashville	TN	615-292-6152
Music City Tattoo	Nashville	TN	615-327-9440
Nashville Quality Tattoo	Nashville	TN	615-228-8681
Queen of Hearts	Nashville	TN	615-256-5051
* Rites of Ascension	Nashville	TN	615-256-5051

* Forever Yours Tattoo Studio	Old Hickory	TN	615-847-1153

Texas

	Custom Tattoos	Arlington	TX	817-274-6561
	Skin Art Gallery	Arlington	TX	817-461-4213
*	Atomic Tattoo & Piercing	Austin	TX	512-458-9693
*	Capitol City Tattoo & Piercing	Austin	TX	512-494-0717
*	Kane and Able Tattoo	Austin	TX	512-472-6669
*	Notorious Ed's Underground Tattoos & Piercing	Austin	TX	512-476-8066
	Singapore John's Tattoo Arcade	Austin	TX	512-440-0075 or 512-835-0007
	Touch of a Feather	Austin	TX	512-396-TATU
	Chuck's Custom Tattooing	Beaumont	TX	409-898-2075
	Tattoo Consortium	Bryan	TX	409-846-7084
*	Onix Subcultures Tattoos & Piercing	Corpus Christi	TX	512-857-6649
	Cybergraph-x	Dallas	TX	214-653-1392
*	Obscurities	Dallas	TX	214-559-3706
	Pair o' Dice Tattoos	Dallas	TX	214-744-DICE
	Pirate Penny's Tattoo Adventure	Dallas	TX	214-343-9525
*	Skin & Bones	Dallas	TX	214-741-4653
	Skin Art Gallery	Dallas	TX	214-387-1755
	Tigger's Body Art	Dallas	TX	214-655-2639
	Trilogy Tattoos	Dallas	TX	214-559-0470
	Tattoos by Bob	Dennison	TX	903-465-1535
	Creative Images	Denton	TX	817-484-5488
	Intradermal Designs	Denton	TX	817-381-5006
	Texas Inkslingers Tattoo	Dumas	TX	806-935-7433
	Flesh Tones	El Paso	TX	915-565-1437
	Renegade Tattoo	El Paso	TX	915-562-8288

Cowtown Tattoo	Ft. Worth	TX	817-624-7973
Mild II Wild Tattoos	Ft. Worth	TX	817-624-4664
Randy Adams Tattoo Studio	Ft. Worth	TX	817-446-0272
Body Language Tattoo Studio	Galveston	TX	409-763-4088
* Russtr's Tattoos & Body Piercing	Harker Heights	TX	817-699-8113
Artistic Design	Houston	TX	713-643-8672
B & B Fine Line	Houston	TX	713-458-8282
Bad Boyz Tattoo	Houston	TX	713-480-0699
Boots' Fine Line	Houston	TX	713-445-9117
Scream'n Demon Tattoos	Houston	TX	713-523-1404
Dave's Master Tattooing	Killeen	TX	817-526-2389
Touch of a Feather	Live Oak	TX	210-590-TATS
Tattoos by Papa-San	Longview	TX	903-234-1151
Ultimate Vision Quest	Lubbock	TX	806-749-8500
Dr. Power's Tattoo	McAllen	TX	210-686-7890
Dave's Tattoo	Odessa	TX	915-368-5603
Tattoo Graphics	Plainview	TX	806-296-6456
Smith's Ink Slingers	Queen City	TX	903-796-3342
Hot Spot	San Angelo	TX	915-659-0928
Tattoos by Laura	San Angelo	TX	915-659-2293
Art Tattoos Fun	San Antonio	TX	210-828-1041
* Backbone Body Modifications	San Antonio	TX	210-349-6637
FO's Tattooing	San Antonio	TX	210-734-5110
Perfection Tattoo	San Antonio	TX	210-736-0506
Phantasy Tattoos	San Antonio	TX	210-590-8036
* Tattoos by Feather Tattoos & Piercing	San Marcos	TX	512-396-TATU
Sheri's Texas Tattoo	Sweetwater	TX	915-236-6234
Dermagraphic Studio	Texarkana	TX	903-793-2276
Purple Dragon	Waxahachie	TX	214-937-1332

A Different Drummer Tattoo	Wichita Falls	TX	817-855-4481

Utah

*	5th Avenue Studio	Murray City	UT	801-263-0500
	Artistic Skin Illustrations	Ogden	UT	801-625-0233
	Susie M's	Ogden	UT	801-627-9181
	Artistic Skin Illustrations	Provo	UT	801-374-8222
	Artistic Skin Illustrations	Salt Lake City	UT	801-446-8863
*	Galaxina	Salt Lake City	UT	801-532-7122
	Susie M's	Salt Lake City	UT	801-467-8282

Vermont

*	Metropolitan Hair	Burlington	VT	802-864-0065

Virginia

	Body Art Tattoos	Berryville	VA	540-955-0111
	Custom Dreams	Blacksburg	VA	540-951-4765
	American Tattooing	Carrollton	VA	804-238-9664
	Flash Tat-2 Worx	Charlottesville	VA	804-293-8998
*	Red Dragon Tattoo & Piercing	Charlottesville	VA	804-295-7784
	TJ's Dermagraphic Tattoos II	Charlottesville	VA	804-979-7733
	Custom Tattoo	Christianburg	VA	540-381-6282
*	Caspian Tattoo	Forest	VA	804-385-8282
	Colorworks	Front Royal	VA	703-636-8282
	Rebel's Tattoo Studio	Front Royal	VA	703-636-9050
*	Body Works Tattooing	Harrisonburg	VA	703-433-2766
	TJ's Dermagraphic Tattoos I	Harrisonburg	VA	540-564-1671
	Personal Expression	Madison Heights	VA	804-528-4570

Exposed Temptations	Manassas	VA	703-335-2134
Altered Images	Petersburg	VA	804-733-3284
Skin Ink & Body Shop	Radford	VA	703-633-1846
Absolute Art Tattoo	Richmond	VA	804-355-8001
Red Dragon Tattoo & Piercing	Richmond	VA	804-230-7908
Rock n Roll Tattoo	Richmond	VA	804-794-8582
* Ancient Art Tattoo & Piercing	Roanoke	VA	540-774-0819
TJ's Dermagraphics III	Staunton	VA	540-885-2804
A-1 Tattooing	Trinagle	VA	702-221-8287
Southern Rose Tattoo	Waynesboro	VA	703-943-5454
Ancient Art Tattoo	Winchester	VA	703-667-9050
State of the Art Tattooing	Winchester	VA	703-667-9050

Washington

Kalamalka Studio	Bellingham	WA	360-733-3832
Mum's Tattoo	Blaine	WA	604-984-7831
Painless Ric's Tattoo Parlor	Camas	WA	360-694-9447
Everett Tattoo Emporium	Everett	WA	425-252-2315
Tattoo Alley	Federal Way	WA	253-946-9447
Tribal Images	Ferndale	WA	360-380-1157
Kent Dermagraphics	Kent	WA	253-852-2550
Kirkland Tattoo Studio	Kirkland	WA	425-828-8815
Mary & Paddy's Tattoos	Longview	WA	360-414-4154
Little City Studios	Palouse	WA	509-878-1917
Tattoo Elegance	Port Angeles	WA	360-457-1131
Class Act Tattoo	Pyallup	WA	253-845-8503
Pate's Perfect Solutions	Redmond	WA	425-869-0343
Custom Skin Design	Richland	WA	509-946-1847
* Atomic Garden Tattoos & Piercing	Seattle	WA	206-632-1695
Body VooDoo Skin Art	Seattle	WA	206-363-7896
Custom Tattoo	Seattle	WA	206-633-0855

George Long at Rudy's Barber Shop	Seattle	WA	206-329-3008
Jerm-N-Dave's Downtown Tattoos	Seattle	WA	206-623-9554
Seattle Tattoo Emporium	Seattle	WA	206-622-6895
* Slave to the Needle Tattoos & Piercing	Seattle	WA	206-789-8288
Tattoo You	Seattle	WA	206-324-6443
* Vanities	Seattle	WA	206-784-7897
Vyvyn's Tattoo	Seattle	WA	206-622-1535
Tiny Tim's Tattoos	Sedro-Woolley	WA	206-855-1739
Electric Dreams	Selah	WA	509-697-7477
Artistic Impressions	Spokane	WA	509-483-6545
Tiger Tattoo	Spokane	WA	509-535-1003
Eagle's Tattoo	Tacoma	WA	253-535-4662
Valley Tattoo	Veradale	WA	509-922-4842
Liquid Dermagraphics	Wenatchee	WA	509-662-4251
Red Dragon	Wenatchee	WA	509-662-1309
Jim & Jenni's Quality Tattoos	Yakima	WA	509-452-8287
Stranger's Tattoo Place	Yakima	WA	509-452-8705

West Virginia

Thinkin Ink	Elkins	WV	304-636-7778
Thinkin Ink	Fairmont	WV	304-366-1279
Personal Art	Keyser	WV	304-788-4559
* TK Dodrill Jewelers	Huntington	WV	304-523-4748
* Eclipse Body Piercing	Martinsburg	WV	304-263-3053
Tat-2's Custom Image	S. Charleston	WV	304-768-4830
Thinkin Ink	Summersville	WV	304-872-1872

Wisconsin

Windy City Tattoos	Eau Claire	WI	715-834-1917
Majestic	Fond du Lac	WI	414-924-4100
Virtual Reality Tattooing	Fond du Lac	WI	414-924-7814
Main Stream	Green Bay	WI	414-435-9988
Skin Illustrations	Green Bay	WI	414-432-3735
* Diamond Ted's Tattoo Studio & Body Piercing	Janesville	WI	608-754-8288
Borderline Tattoo	Kenosha	WI	414-694-4009
Night Breed Tattoo	Kenosha	WI	414-884-9667
Main Street Tattoo	Kewaskum	WI	414-626-4445
* Steve's Tattoo & Body Piercing	Madison	WI	608-251-6111
Ultimate Arts	Madison	WI	608-249-7352
Doc's Tattoo	Medford	WI	715-748-3558
Absolute Tattooing	Menomonee Falls	WI	414-255-4884
Cherokee Chuck's Tattoos	Mukwonago	WI	414-363-8281
Accents in Ink	Oak Creek	WI	414-762-6424
Ink Stains	Racine	WI	414-637-3485
Absolute Tattooing	Sheboygan	WI	414-457-6771
Permanent Skin Art	Siren	WI	715-349-2046
* Ink Spot Tattoo & Piercing	Stevens Point	WI	715-344-6453
Black Dragon Tattoo	Waukesha	WI	414-521-1177

Wyoming

Skibo's Tattoo	Cheyenne	WY	307-632-6869
Evening Shade Dermagraphics	Gillette	WY	307-686-1363
Modern Art Dermagraphics	Rock Springs	WY	307-382-5247

Argentina

American Tattoo Studio	Buenos Aires	0541-8157032
Gabriel, Katzaroff	Rosario	0541-499474

Australia

*	Primal Urge Piercing	Perth	09-3211909
	Wizards of Ink	Albury, NSW	610-60253899
	Pleasure & Pain Tattoo	Allawah, NSW	610-25881169
	Pete's Place	Bathurst, NSW	610-63321544
	South Coast Tattoo	Corrimal, NSW	610-42837135
*	Stu-Art Body Piercing	Dubbo, NSW	+06-8818677
	Ancient Warrior	Emerton, NSW	610-26289934
	Skin Deep Body Art	Granville, NSW	610-26077635
	Pete & Max's	Kings Cross, NSW	610-23573223
	Sleevemasters Tattoo	Kings Cross, NSW	610-23114162
	Creative Tattoo Art	Lismore, NSW	610-66218020
	Duchy & Son	Liverpool, NSW	610-26027139
	Jill Mounsey	Mangerton, NSW	610-42265232
	Bank Corner Tattoo	Newcastle, NSW	610-49263072
	Tom & Brads Tattooing	Newcastle, NSW	610-49291400
	War Paint Tattoo	St. Marys, NSW	610-26733155
*	Polymorph Body Art	St. Peters, NSW	+02-5198923
	Illustrated Man Tattoo Studio	Sydney, NSW	610-22113761
	Kiwi Kim's Celtic Dragon Tattoo Art	Sydney, NSW	610-25165120
	Skin Art by Griz	Taree, NSW	610-65510742
	Expert Tattooing by Andre	Brisbane, QLD	610-73913264
	Kustom Tattoos by Little Mick	Brisbane, QLD	610-72528881
	Outback Tattooing	Mount Isa, QLD	610-77495188
	Eternal Graphics Tattoo	Slackscreek, QLD	07-8089184
	Four Roses Tattoo	Adelaide, South	610-2313044

Skin Art Tattoo	Mowbray, TAS	610-03266438
Splash of Color	Ascot Vale, VIC	610-33754169
Jed Hill	Beaufort, VIC	610-53492139
Tattoo City	Dandenong, VIC	610-37948809
Warm Art Studio	Essendon Melbourne, VIC	610-3375728
Bodyline Tattooing	Frankstown, VIC	610-37814381
Ink Spot III	Geelong, VIC	052-232887
Rocky's Dungeon	Geelong, VIC	610-52294114
Lifelong Design Tattoo	Glenroy, VIC	610-33066323
Universal Tattooing	Hastings, VIC	610-59792273
* Body Language Tattoo/Piercing	Lilydale, VIC	610-87355884
* The Piercing Urge	Manscape Melbourne, VIC	03-530-2244
Tattoo Art	Oak Park, VIC	610-33002988
Fantasy Art Tattoo	Pakenham, VIC	610-59413429
Ink City Tattooing	Preston, VIC	610-44705996
Bridge Rd. Tattoo Studio	Richmond, VIC	610-34288542
Ballarat Body Art	Sebastapol, VIC	610-53361018
Ace Tattooing	St. Albans, VIC	610-45367749
Skin Deep	Traralgon, VIC	610-51761088
Mainline Tattooing	Victoria, VIC	610-35849678
Patsy Farrow Tattooing	W. Footscray, VIC	610-33141203
Moving Pictures	Williamstown, VIC	610-53976279
Applecross Tattoo	Applecross, Western	09-3161328
Pearl Coast Tattooing	Broome, Western	09-935204

Austria

Hot Vienna Tattoo	Eing.Jagdg	02264/40 612
Colourbox	Feldkirch-Altenstadt	05522/71 717
Custom Tattooing by Mario Barth	Graz	03169/12 845
Leguan Tattoo	Neustadt	02622/65 165

| Tattoos by Stone | Leoben | 03842/47 643 |

Belgium

| Art Line Tattoo | Brugge | 050-392154 |
| Tattoos by Rinto | Groningen | 050-126607 |

Brazil

Casa Dos Dragoes	Cabo Frio, RJ	0246-45-4123
Marcio Tattoo	São Paulo	0132-38-9514
Polaco Tattoo Shop	São Paulo	011-222-8049

Canada

Eternal Image Tattoo	Calgary, Alberta	403-228-3958
Joker's Wild	Calgary, Alberta	403-230-3529
Smilin' Buddha Tattoo	Calgary, Alberta	403-242-5922
To the Point	Calgary, Alberta	403-240-2120
Bear's Skin Art Tattoos	Edmonton, Alberta	403-482-3876
Gem Tattooing	Edmonton, Alberta	403-477-2116
Ink Machine	Edmonton, Alberta	403-423-0267
Roy & Sharon's	Edmonton, Alberta	403-477-8381
Tattoos by Joey & The Bear	Edmonton, Alberta	403-433-6514
Top Gun Tattoo	Edmonton, Alberta	403-444-1059
Zipps Tattooing	Edmonton, Alberta	403-439-0519
Splashing Ink	Fort Macleod, Alberta	403-553-4266
Dansing Dragon Tattoos	Medicine Hat, Alberta	403-526-1950
Fantasy Tattoo	Abbotsford, British Columbia	604-852-4609
Mirella's Touch of Class	Burnaby, British Columbia	604-430-6067
Anarchy Ink	Campbell River, British Columbia	604-286-0713

Brian's Tattoo	Clearbrook, British Columbia	604-850-2379
Comox Valley Tattoo	Courtenay, British Columbia	604-338-9599
Tigger Tatz Tattoo Parlour	Cranbrook, British Columbia	604-426-6990
Trippindicular	Ft. St. John, British Columbia	604-785-1232
Skin Art Tattooing	Golden, British Columbia	604-344-5869
Bob's Tattoos	Kelowna, British Columbia	604-868-0405
Ritual Tattoo	Kelowna, British Columbia	604-862-8205
Tattoos by JoAnn	Kelowna, British Columbia	604-860-8822
Lady Luck Tattoo	Langley, British Columbia	604-533-6683
Tattoo Emporium	Nanaimo, British Columbia	604-754-0117
Tattoos by Raz	Nelson, British Columbia	604-354-1755
Dutchman Tattoos	New Westminister, British Columbia	604-522-5156
New West Tattoo	New Westminister, British Columbia	604-522-3004
	Mum's Tattoo N. Vancouver, British Columbia	604-984-7831
** Canadian Assoc. of Professional Tattooists	Revelstoke, British Columbia	604-837-2645
Shambala Tattoos	Revelstoke, British Columbia	604-837-2645
Royal City Tattoos	Sapperton, British Columbia	604-540-6944
Dragon Tattoo	Surrey, British Columbia	604-582-7222

Golden Lion Tattoo	Surrey, British Columbia	604-583-4609
Spider Tattoo	Surrey, British Columbia	604-582-1191
Tattoos by Raz	Surrey, British Columbia	604-638-2042
Ace Tattoo	Vancouver, British Columbia	604-253-4922
Anarchy Ink	Vancouver, British Columbia	604-689-7789
Body Branding	Vancouver, British Columbia	604-669-5714
Devil's Den	Vancouver, British Columbia	604-669-1422
Native Images Tattoo	Vancouver, British Columbia	604-879-1895
Sacred Heart Tattoo Gallery	Vancouver, British Columbia	604-224-1149
West Coast Tattoo	Vancouver, British Columbia	604-681-2049
Vernon Tattoo	Vernon, British Columbia	604-545-3325
Tattoo Emporium	Victoria, British Columbia	604-383-2455
Tattoo Zoo	Victoria, British Columbia	604-361-1952
Universal Tattooing	Victoria, British Columbia	604-382-9417
Warlock Tattoo	Brandon, Manitoba	204-727-8818
Artistic Tattooing	Winnipeg, Manitoba	204-253-7449
René's Tattoos	Winnipeg, Manitoba	204-475-5566
Skin Dimensions	Winnipeg, Manitoba	204-478-3513
Tattoos by Strider	Winnipeg, Manitoba	204-235-0453
Winnepeg's Finest	Winnipeg, Manitoba	204-284-1814
Tattoos for the Individual	Winnipeg, Manitoba	204-774-8956
Krystal Blade Tattoo	Fredericton, New Brunswick	506-451-1417

Red Lion	Oromocto, New Brunswick	506-446-5894
China Grove	St. John, New Brunswick	506-633-2202
Merchant Marie's	Dartmouth, Nova Scotia	902-463-9685
Black Rose Tattoo	Halifax, Nova Scotia	902-429-8822
Sailor Jerry's Tattoo	Halifax, Nova Scotia	902-425-1695
Pushin Inc.	Barrie, Ontario	705-728-8282
Tattoos by Tim	Barrie, Ontario	705-737-2257
Baby Lu's Fine Tattooing	Brampton, Ontario	905-790-9499
El Toro Tattooing	Brampton, Ontario	519-758-8282
Nightwind Tattoo	Brampton, Ontario	905-456-2141
* Exotic Body Piercing	Brantford, Ontario	519-758-8242
Requiem II	Brantford, Ontario	519-756-7366
Joe's Custom Tattooing	Cambridge, Ontario	519-621-0345
Adventure Tattoo	Carleton, Ontario	905-897-0500
Body Graphics Tattoo	Carleton, Ontario	613-257-4312
Mississauga Tattoo	Cooksville, Ontario	905-270-5527
El Toro Tattooing	Cornwall, Ontario	613-932-0740
Tattoo Sanctuary	Dunville, Ontario	905-774-5594
Dermagraphics by Paul Vicary	Guelph, Ontario	519-836-8680
Nighthawk Tattoo	Guelph, Ontario	519-767-0801
Allstyle Tattoo	Hamilton, Ontario	905-527-6790
Barber Shoppe Body Art	Hamilton, Ontario	905-312-4929
Squirrel's Skin Art	Hamilton, Ontario	416-575-4210
Express U Tattoo	Kingston, Ontario	613-541-1770
Elsewhere Designs	Kitchener, Ontario	519-742-1020
Tattoo Art	Kitchener, Ontario	519-576-8054
Blue Dragon Tattoo	London, Ontario	519-434-4706
Finesse Tattoo Works	London, Ontario	519-661-0599
Tattoo Shop	London, Ontario	519-234-1144

Tattoos Unltd	London, Ontario	519-672-8025
13th Generation Tattoo	Niagara Falls, Ontario	905-374-8455
Down East Tattooing	Niagara Falls, Ontario	905-358-9100
Way Cool Tattoo	Niagara Falls, Ontario	905-374-8116
Wilde Tattoo	North Bay, Ontario	705-495-6694
Stews Tattoos	Oakville, Ontario	905-825-9165
Right in the Skin	Oshawa, Ontario	905-432-9165
Blue's Tattoo	Ottawa, Ontario	613-232-6179
Future Skin	Ottawa, Ontario	613-562-8282
Game Day Tattoos	Ottawa, Ontario	613-562-0376
Kreator Tattoo	Ottawa, Ontario	613-567-7398
Living Colour Tattoo	Ottawa, Ontario	613-729-9310
New Moon Tattoo	Ottawa, Ontario	613-596-1790
Sleeping Dragon Tattoo Emporium	Ottawa, Ontario	613-744-1591
Wizzard's Den	Petawawa, Ontario	613-687-5250
Taylor's Tattoo	Peterborough, Ontario	705-748-4290
Skin Graphics	Port Colborne, Ontario	905-835-5115
Body Designs	Ridgeway, Ontario	905-894-4533
Drifter's Ink Well	Sault Ste. Marie, Ontario	705-945-5278
Twin Cities Tattoo	Sault Ste. Marie, Ontario	705-256-5446
Creative Skin Art	Scarborough, Ontario	416-266-5702
Lower East Side Tattoo	Scarborough, Ontario	416-267-7300
Voodoo Tattoo	Scarborough, Ontario	416-693-1146
Jay's Tattoo Fantasy	Southpick, Ontario	905-831-0905
Artistic Impressions	St. Catherines, Ontario	905-687-6913
Boundless Ecstasy	St. Catherines, Ontario	905-682-3822
Cutting Edge	St. Catherines, Ontario	905-684-2422
Canadian Dragon Tattoo	Sudbury, Ontario	705-688-7008
Stray Katz	Sudbury, Ontario	705-671-8013
Lone Wolfe Tattoos	Thorold, Ontario	905-680-1044
Living Colour	Thunder Bay, Ontario	807-622-7713
Abstract Arts	Toronto, Ontario	416-777-1244
Accents of Skin	Toronto, Ontario	416-537-4821
Artatak	Toronto, Ontario	416-463-9581

Artatorture	Toronto, Ontario	416-363-1167
Beachcombers Tattoo	Toronto, Ontario	416-532-9481
* New Tribe Tattoo & Piercing	Toronto, Ontario	416-977-2786
Pluto's Place	Toronto, Ontario	416-503-4513
Realism Tattoo	Toronto, Ontario	416-424-1399
Studio One	Toronto, Ontario	416-466-8000
* Urban Primitives Tattoo & Piercing	Toronto, Ontario	416-966-9155
Way Cool Tattoos	Toronto, Ontario	416-603-0145
Squirrel's Skin Art	Wellington, Ontario	905-575-4210
Sinful Inflictions	Whitby, Ontario	905-430-9840
Body Language Tattoo	Windsor, Ontario	519-252-8404
Tattoo Shop	Windsor, Ontario	519-977-1034
World of Tattoos	Windsor, Ontario	519-944-6406
Quebec Tatoo	Quebec	418-640-0715
Tattoo Voodoo	Granby, Quebec	514-375-6960
* Azriel's Tattoo & Body Piercing	Montreal, Quebec	514-525-2639
Julio Tattoos	Montreal, Quebec	514-421-7408
Pt. St. Charles Tattoo Co.	Montreal, Quebec	514-931-2325
Tatouage Artistique	Montreal, Quebec	514-529-8288
Tatouage du Quebec	Montreal, Quebec	514-521-5375
Tatouage Iris	Montreal, Quebec	514-526-8060
Quebec Tattoo	Quebec City, Quebec	514-931-2325
Vision Tattoo	Quebec City, Quebec	514-648-6224
Riff Raff Tattoo	La Ronge, Saskatchewan	306-352-1568
Rising Sun Tattoo & Piercing	Regina, Saskatchewan	306-525-4585
Valhalla Tattoos	Regina, Saskatchewan	306-352-1568
Fantasies for Flesh	Saskatoon, Saskatchewan	306-244-0812
Saskatoon Fine Line	Saskatoon, Saskatchewan	306-242-3476
Tattoo Shop	Saskatoon, Saskatchewan	306-652-3232
* Ye Olde Clip Joint	Unit, Saskatchewan	306-228-3977

Denmark

Artistic Tattooing	Aalborg	98 13 89 19
Frank & Co.	Aarhus	86 12 89 23
Tattooing by Danny & Bimbo	Copenhagen	33 15 90 86
Henning Jorgensen	Elsinore	49 20 25 29
Royal Tattoo	Helsingor	45 49 20 27 70
* Weber Tattoo & Piercing	Naestved	53 72 53 53

Dutch Caribbean

Professional Tattoos	Oranjestad, Aruba	297-8-36602

Finland

Duck's Tattoo Studio	Helsinki	693-1319
Tattoo Art by Andrey	Helsinki	777-2784

France

Graphicaderme	Avignon	90 82 32 90
Derma Folies	Bordeaux	56 51 61 21
Michael's Tattoos	Bordeaux	33 565 16650
Michel Tattoo 'n' Family	Bordeaux	56 44 27 25
Dream Ink Tattoo Studio	Mulhouse	89 42 53 77
Miss Pic	Nîmes	66 67 61 76
Tatou Surveaux	Paray le Monial	03 85 81 42 49
* Gauntlet	Paris	47 00 73 60
Prestige Tattoo	Paris	45 94 56 34
Tatoage Bernard	Paris	45 32 06 44
Tin Tin Tatouage	Paris	48 05 14 89
Shark's Tattoo	St. Etienne	77 33 37 17
Asphalt Jungle	Strasbourg	88 22 23 24

Germany

Alf Diamond's FTA Tattoo	Aschaffenburg	69 617 592
Kalle's Tattoo Shop	Bamberg	095 127 379
Hango's Tattoo	Berlin	030 344 4112
Hawwi Tattoo	Berlin	030 686 5699
Tattoo Paradise	Berlin	030 391 8744
Coma Tattoo	Bottrop	0 20 41/26 32 52
Sting's Tätowierstudio	Bremerhaven	0471 20 72 01
Tattoo Studio	Dortmund	0231 83 84 97
Alex Tattoo Atelier	Ehningen	07034 8971
Dead Rebel Tattoo	Frankfurt	064 171 655
Skin Deep Body Art	Hagen	02331 18 28 99
* Endless Pain Tattoo & Piercing	Hamburg	040 31-01-70
Tattoo Lin by Sven	Hamburg	040 6773835
Exclusive Tattoos	Hebelweg	0791-52478
* Crazy Greg's Tattoo & Piercing	Heidelberg	06221 168338
Alf Diamond's FTA Tattoo	Kaiserlautern	0631-13451
Tattoo Center Studio	Koblenz	0261 210530
Major Tom's Tattoo	Kornwestheim	07154 26785
Ralph's Tattoo	Lorrach	07621-10347
Achim's Fine Line Art	Ludenscheid	02351 380999
Peter's Tattoo	Manheim	0621-377619
Rainbow Tattoo	Munich	089-188580
Sohne Tattoo	Munich	089 521529
Tattoos by Don	Oberursel	061 71 59411
Doc's Tattoo	Salzgitter	05341-15854
Monique's Tattoos	Wiesbaden	061 130 5891

Hungary

Ballarat Body Art	Sebastopol	053-36-1018

Israel

Tattooing by Nathan	Haifa	04-523282
Johnny Two-Thumb Tattoo	Tel Aviv	03-5270416

Italy

Anomina Tatuaggi	Manerbio	030-9938681
* I-Max International	Riccione	0541-642-160

Netherlands

Amsterdam Tattooing	Amsterdam	020-620-6932
Hanky Panky Tattooing	Amsterdam	020-627-4848
Skin Deep	Amsterdam	020-638-8590
Tattoos by Molly	Amsterdam	020-420-4035
Tattoo Bob	Breda	076-22-72-52
Studio Tattoo Mick	Dordrecht	078 631 08 55
Dragon Tattoo	Eindhoven	040 461679
Herco, Roelofs	Olst	05708-1275
Future Art Tattoo Studio	Rotterdam	010-48-7539
Frenky The Hague Tattoo	Den Haag	070-364 30 30
Marco Bratt Tattoo	Scheveningen	070-350 75 77

New Zealand

* Body Piercing Specialties	Auckland	01-952-0675
Downunder Tattooing	Christchurch	064-33843910
Tattoo Alley	Christchurch	377-1828
Dynamic Dermagraphics	Waihi	07-863-6376

* Flesh Wound, Manakau	Levin	06-362-6694
Roger Ingerton's Tattoo Art	Wellington	0845-242

Panama

Panama Tattoo Studio	Panama City	507-260-9716

Puerto Rico

Demon Ed, Voronezh	Bopomem	073-234-6582
Storm Riders	Old San Juan	809-721-4202

Singapore

Johnny Two-Thumb Tattoo	Singapore	7374861

South Africa

Duck's Tattoo	Cape Town	021-434-4400
Ink Wizard	Boksburg, Johannesburg	011-826-2221
CJ's Professional Tattoo	Edenvale, Johannesburg	011-616-7489
Tattoo Trend	Linden, Johannesburg	011-782-7430
Mystique Tattoo	Melville, Johannesburg	011-726-2038
Little Angels Tattoo Studio	Northcliffe, Johannesburg	011-678-0606
Wayne's Tattoos	West Turfontien, Johannesburg	011-434-2362
Rudy's Tattoo Studio	Sunnyside, Pretoria	012-314-8744

Spain

Mao & Kathy Tattoo	Madrid	5944956

Big Wave Tattoo	Torrelavega	9422892757

Sweden

Skinnfantasi Tatuering	Johanneshov	08-686-08-43
Viking Tattoo Studio	Linköping	013-13 06 82
Doc Holiday's	Öbebro	019 10 21 35
Boije's Tattoo	Stockholm	08-530 604670
Flash Fighter Studio	Stockholm	08-18-17 87
Clifford's Tattoo	Sundevall	060569118

Switzerland

Basel Tattoo	Basel	061 281 063
Tattoo Shop	Fribourg	037 243695
Tattoos by Nicox	Geneva	022 13493790
Hot Flash Tattoos	Luzern	041-22-67 67
Orlando's Tattoo	Muttenz	061-61-62 54
Varry's Tattoo Shop	Sissach	061-98-12 12
Howy's Tattoo	St. Gallen	071-24-16 36
Hammer Joe Tattoo	Zurich	01-242-5042
Ink Funatics	Zurich	01-261-9080

United Kingdom

Brent's Viking Tattoo	Bedfordshire, England	0582 663749
Ian of Reading	Berkshire, England	01734 598616
Dragon Images	Bilston, England	0902405995
Reaperz	Birmingham, England	021-457 8982
Skin Deep Tattoo	Bristol, England	0272 413 447
Steve Potton	Cheshire, England	01457 863129
Celtic Art Tattoo	Derby, England	0246 235176
Tattoo Factory	Devon, England	0626 60921
Tattoo Magic	Dorset, England	01305 770279
* Wildcat Collection	East Sussex, England	0273 323758

Colchester Tattoo	Essex, England	01296 766810
George Bone Tattoo	Hanwell, England	081 579 0831
Spectrum	Isle of Man, England	672256
Pictures on Skin	Kent, England	0634 578036
Inkspirations	Lancashire, England	01254-388353
** Assoc. of Professional Tattoo Artists	London, England	081-444-8779
Ben Gunn	London, England	181 529 1132
Evil from the Needle	London, England	071 482 2412
Into You	London, England	0171 253 5085
Lal Hardy	London, England	081-444 8779
New Wave Tattoos	London, England	081-444-8779
Sims Tattoos	London, England	081-656-2248
Skin Graphics by Mick	London, England	081-859-1901
Inkspirations	Manchester, England	161 787 7827
Tattootime	Nottingham, England	0115 9736308
Dragon Ink	Oxford, England	0865 728492
Ink Wizard	Portsmouth, England	01705 793845
Unique Tattooing	Portsmouth, England	0822105
Tattoo Magic by John Williams	Southampton, England	0703 33 1470
Custom Tattoo	Surrey, England	081 546 1010
Brian Carville Tattooing	Windsor, England	0753-867-447
Ink Castle	Belfast, Ireland	0232 242167
Leonardo's Tattoo	Cork, Ireland	021-314622
Island Tattoo	Isle of Wight, Ireland	0983 613013
Dragon's Lair	Edinburgh, Scotland	031 3468566
Terry Tattoo	Glasgow, Scotland	041-552-5740
Abracadabra Tattoo	Gwent, Wales	0443 837410
Redskin Tattoo	Gwynedd, Wales	01758 614350